ONCE AROUND
THE PLANET

ONCE AROUND THE PLANET

RUNNING 24,902 MILES

DOUG RICHARDS

First published by Pitch Publishing, 2023

Pitch Publishing
9 Donnington Park,
85 Birdham Road,
Chichester,
West Sussex,
PO20 7AJ
www.pitchpublishing.co.uk
info@pitchpublishing.co.uk

ISBN 978 1 80150 169 9

Typesetting and origination by Pitch Publishing
Printed and bound in Great Britain by TJ Books, Padstow

Contents

Dedicated to the memory of Elizabeth

(Lizzie) Tovey, 1973–2020.

Courage beyond words.

RUN LIZZIE RUN

Chapter 1

The ebbs and flows of Venice

THE AFTERNOON sunshine glinted off its polished, metal surface and tears of pride welled in my eyes. In my right hand, held aloft, as I waved with my other arm to the vociferous crowds of spectators lining the pavements, was one of the most precious items I had ever been privileged to carry. It was Her Majesty Queen Elizabeth II's Baton and I had been selected as one of a chosen few who would carry it on its worldwide journey in the lead-up to the 2022 Commonwealth Games in Birmingham.

Yes, it was only a 200m slow jog, but not every run is defined by distance travelled and time taken. No run has ever filled me with more personal pride than this one did. I took my time. I wasn't going to rush that treasured moment.

But why me? I am a naturally modest person who doesn't like to blow my own trumpet. Why had I been picked out from the many thousands of deserving nominees to have the honour of carrying the Queen's

Baton? As much as I have relished the experiences my own back catalogue of worldwide running adventures has given me, and am proud of the tens of thousands of pounds I have raised for charities in the process, perhaps the greatest pleasure I get is from inspiring others to embark on their own running journey. It may be a young child who, having listened to one of my school talks, decides to sign up for junior parkrun. Or maybe an octogenarian who bravely attends one of my couch to 5k programmes and then, nine weeks later, I can marvel at the smile on their face as they achieve their goal. And yes, my written and spoken words have also gone on to inspire others to achieve even greater heights; half- and full marathons and even some of the toughest ultra-runs our planet has to offer.

Running, in so many ways, has played a pivotal role in my life journey, and those few, priceless, emotional, baton-bearing minutes seemed to encapsulate all the many facets of joy this simple activity has provided for me.

* * *

It was during the summer of 1981 that I had taken that very first step out of my front door with the single goal of running for a mile. Quite simply, I wanted to begin to reverse the decline in my physical fitness, even though I was only 33 years old at the time. That moment represented one of the most momentous decisions of my life and would shape it for decades to come.

If you had stopped me then and listed the places I would eventually run in, I would have laughed at you. If you had stopped me then and told me of the adventures that were ahead of me, and of the amazing people I would share them with, I would have believed you were living in some kind of fantasy world. If you had stopped me then and told me that the amazing journey I was about to embark on would provide enough material to write not one, but two books, I would have doubted your sanity. For goodness sake, all I was going to do was to run around the block, and hope that the inevitable pain that I knew I would feel at the end of the run did not put me off running for life.

Now I sit at my keyboard, preparing to begin yet another journal of this extraordinary journey that I have been privileged enough to enjoy, and occasionally suffer. A trilogy! Who would have believed it?

My first book, *Running Hot & Cold*, takes you back to the very beginning, not just that one-mile run, but why it took me into my fourth decade to discover that I enjoyed running. Life is an unpredictable journey; we never quite know what lies around the next corner, and the direction my running life took was very much intertwined with the roller-coaster experiences of family, health and work matters. I openly admit that, at various points in my life, I have suffered with mental wellbeing issues, principally anxiety and depression, and I will never undervalue the role that running has played in helping me keep things in perspective. Nothing boosts your self-confidence more than achieving a goal that the little voice in your head was saying was beyond your capability.

My first book traced the journey from that first run to half- and full marathons, and eventually to ultra-marathons. I explored new cities by running around them, and then felt this strange urge to explore races that, frankly, no rational person would want to run in. This led me to discover the mountains and deserts of China and the humidity and jungles of Sri Lanka. I shared African plains with the native wildlife, and battled my way through the barren winter landscapes of Siberia and the polar ice cap in Greenland. In contrast, the searing heat of the Sahara would test me to my very limits.

In the sequel, *Can We Run With You, Grandfather?*, I described a scenic return to south-east Asia in the Bagan region of Myanmar which preceded a first visit to South America for a half-marathon in Rio de Janeiro, and this opened up an enticing new goal. Could I run at least a half-marathon on each of Earth's seven continents before I reached the age of 70? There were a few trials and tribulations along the way, but the answer was yes. The contrasting conditions of the heat of the Australian Outback and the wind and blizzards of Antarctica saw me earn the seven continents accolade that would have been beyond my wildest dreams when I first set out almost 40 years earlier.

* * *

So, that's it. Job done. Seven continents, seven decades. End of; except it wasn't.

What could possibly exceed the magical moments I experienced on the Antarctica trip? Not just the run itself, but the otherworldly scenery, the proximity to and extraordinary interactions with the wildlife, the sea journey across the Drake Passage, the camaraderie on board our ship. The answer is that it probably won't be exceeded, but is that reason enough to stop exploring different horizons?

The simple fact was that, although I was now into my eighth decade, I was blessed with a mind, heart and legs that were still at their happiest when I was out running. I've never been the fastest of runners, but neither have I been among the tailenders. I guess I'm a middle-of-the-pack Joe Average although, as time goes on, there is an inevitable slowing. I know the day will come when I can't do it any more but while I can still run with a smile on my face and not a grimace, the journey will continue.

For me there has to be a goal: something to aim for. It may just be an entry in a local race which gives an incentive to guide the training to ensure you reach race day in the best condition possible to achieve the distance you've set yourself. Longer-term goals are very important too. For the previous couple of years, seven continents had been my target, but now that had been achieved I needed something else: a distant objective far away on the horizon that would help motivate me to get out and run on those days when just any other type of activity seemed a better idea.

As I've said before, I am a shameless obsessive when it comes to recording my runs, even going back to that very first mile. Other than a short period when I was working in London in the late 1990s, when a group of us used to go out and run in Regent's Park at lunchtime, I have meticulously recorded every running journey. Part of me still doesn't understand why I didn't make note of those lunch-break jaunts, but life was very hectic at the time as I was commuting to London from the south coast and had responsibility for my two children at home, so I guess time was a factor. It was also a period when we didn't have wrist-worn GPS devices that could measure how far we had run, and zig-zagging repeatedly around a park would be hard to estimate from a map alone. What it does do, in retrospect, is to give me a little buffer in that whatever mileage milestones I may claim to have achieved, I know in my own mind that I have actually done a little bit more. Anyway, I digress. Long-term targets.

When I crossed the finish line of the Antarctica half-marathon, my cumulative total mileage stood at 19,925. Yes, I am sad, aren't I? That meant I had a little less than 5,000 miles to reach, what for me, would be a magical total of 24,902 miles, the distance of the circumference of our world at the equator: once around the planet. Every time I go out to run, I am nibbling away at that distance, reducing it mile by mile. As I run, I picture my globe in the lounge at home and see myself on that imaginary line, edging towards that target. OK, I may be running across the Pacific Ocean, but it's that goal that keeps me going.

* * *

Once the hullabaloo had died down after the Antarctica trip, my attention turned to a new overseas challenge, one that was causing me quite a bit of anxiety – the Venice Marathon in October of 2018. I have run dozens of marathons before, so why should it make me anxious? As you now know, my primary reason for continuing my running career is enjoyment. Not time, not pace, but just being out there. As time has gone on, and as I have grown older, my enjoyment of the marathon distance has diminished. Not really the race itself as the crowd support on a big-city marathon can normally carry you through. It's really the long training runs to try and get yourself to the fitness level required that can be a challenge. I'm quite selfish when it comes to long training runs with other people and prefer to do them on my own. If your partner or partners are a little faster than you, you can feel yourself being dragged along at a pace you're not comfortable with and vice versa. I just want to run at a pace my body wants to run at on that particular day.

I'd also discovered that advancing years had brought an increasing tendency to calf cramping in the later stages of the long runs, despite using tried and tested fuelling strategies that had worked for me over the years. Half-marathons, no problem; they were probably my favourite distance. I could train for them, run them and feel fully recovered within an hour of crossing the finish line, but my love of the full 26.2-mile distance had decreased over the years.

There is no denying, however, that the marathon is the blue riband event of the distance running world. You know me and my propensity for setting goals to drive on into the future. At some point in recent years, and I do not remember exactly when, although wine was probably a factor, I had announced to my family that I wanted to run one more marathon after I reached the age of 70. Chris, my son, had not forgotten this and so plans were laid that he and I would run the 2018 Venice Marathon and we would turn it into a family break, being joined in this unique city by his wife Lynne, and young Holly who, as their life unfolded, now preferred to be known as Cam. My previous outing over the distance had been back in 2012, in Rome, when I also ran with Chris or, more accurately, behind him. I had taken on the run at short notice when one of Chris's RAF colleagues had pulled out, and was hopelessly under-prepared, having run nothing further than the half-marathon distance beforehand, but I made it. If I could do it then, with a summer ahead to prepare, I could do it again in Venice.

* * *

The summer of 2018 bubbled along nicely. In August I booked my next long-distance running trip, a half-marathon on the remote Easter Island in the South Pacific, to be followed by a few days of sightseeing in Machu Picchu in Peru, a place I had long wanted to visit. This time I would have local company as well. Two months previously I had given one of my running talks to a mixed audience of running friends and inmates at a local open prison. I had mentioned the future possibility of running on Easter Island and a running friend, Clare, who had been in the audience, asked if I would mind if she joined me on the trip. Clare was also very eager to visit Machu Picchu, but her husband Bill would not have been able to cope with the altitude, so this trip would possibly be her only opportunity.

All was going well on the health front apart from becoming rather hard of hearing, particularly in my left ear, which is, I guess, another consequence of advancing years. Curiously, my hearing tended to worsen as the day went on, before reverting back to as near normal as it would get the following morning. As I watched television I would subconsciously be tweaking up the volume control during the day, only to be nearly blown off my sofa the next morning when I turned the TV back on. Eventually, after a few tests, I was given hearing aids for both ears, although I preferred not to wear them for running in case they bounced out, which could incur expensive replacement costs. I just had to make sure that anybody I was running with ran on the good ear side, assuming of course that I wanted to hear what they were saying!

The partial hearing loss also had an impact on some of my longer training runs. In the past, with preferring to do them on my own, I would have sailed off down the narrow country lanes of Worcestershire and Warwickshire (I live on the border). This meant I had to be acutely aware of approaching traffic, which became more challenging with the hearing defect, so I sought new, and safer, routes. Fortunately the town of Redditch, where I live, has a vast network of footpaths and cycle paths, underpasses and flyovers, which make it possible to run long distances without ever having to encounter traffic. It could almost have been designed by a runner, and even now, after 24 years of living there, I am discovering new safe routes.

* * *

On Saturday, 8 September 2018, just seven weeks before the date of the Venice event, I ran a marathon, but of a very different kind. One of our local Arrow Valley parkrun heroes, Kevin, organised an annual charity event which involved running eight different 5km parkrun routes, plus one junior 2km parkrun course, in a single day; 42km in total – yes, a marathon distance, but a very different type of challenge. A coach was provided to transport us between the various venues, although some preferred to use their own cars, and an amazing selection of food and drink was laid on by Rachel, our local parkrun event director's wife. Of course, being a Saturday, only one of the parkruns could start at 9am and be counted as official, the remainder counting as freedom runs.

The day began with a 7.45am start at Sandwell Valley. One of the local team had kindly got up early to explain the route to us but, of course, there would be no marshals. With over 40 of us running, of varying capabilities, we soon spread out and on a twisting course of mixed surfaces, one or two wrong turns were made! However, despite a bit of early morning stiffness in my thigh, a slightly over-distance 3.3 miles was recorded and we leapt on to the coach for the next stage.

Sutton Park was the official parkrun and this was a challenging route, with several tricky climbs and grazing cattle as spectators, a bit too close for some. By the time we reached run three at Perry Hall, rain had begun to fall. This was a fairly flat route which I was familiar with, having run it several times before, and the local core team not only left signs and marshals out from their 9am parkrun, but also provided us with cake and hot drinks – a great gesture, so typical of the parkrun community.

Cannon Hill parkrun was next, another route I knew well, and the rain had now stopped. With a slightly longer break for us to get a bit of lunch, we moved on to Brueton Park, and a different start and finish to the usual to spare us a long walk from the coach drop-off point, but a full 5km all the same. Five parkruns in the bag.

Number six was a bit surreal – a sort of ghost parkrun. It was in the village of Wythall, bordering Birmingham and Solihull, and in the pre-event planning had been advertised as a 'secret' parkrun. The reason for this was that although Wythall Park was a venue recognised by the national parkrun organisation, and had an accurately measured course, only one parkrun was ever held there, as hostility from some members of the local community was so great, with concerns about parking and damage to the grass. We therefore crept from our coach somewhat furtively, looking out for shifting net curtains, just in case the more hostile residents noticed that the runners were back.

Some of us, not myself, had run the one and only Wythall parkrun, so knew the route, but there was a problem. Some sort of local event was going on in the park and, where the start would have been, an archery range had been set up. As we were an unwanted presence anyway, we were certainly not prepared to risk flying arrows, so chose a start point at random and headed off into the outer reaches of the park to run the rest of the prescribed course. There was a consequence to this, of course. When we arrived at the official finishing line, where the timers were waiting to record us, we were all around half a kilometre short of the full distance. Fortunately the finish line was adjacent to a rugby pitch: cue a few dozen runners randomly zig-zagging and circling across the pitch, their faces glued to their running watches until the distance reached the magic 5km, when they could safely run across the line. We didn't wait around after our last runner had finished, and there were definitely a few twitching curtains as we made our way back to the coach.

Stratford-upon-Avon was the next stop and, as in previous years on this annual event, their team pulled out all the stops to make sure our increasingly fatigued bodies were refreshed as much as possible. By now, a few of us had called it a day and complaining muscles were being massaged back to life. There was an interesting question doing the rounds. Which is harder – running a marathon without any rest breaks, or doing it in

5km segments but suffering in between as tired limbs stiffened up in the cramped conditions on the coach? Opinion was fairly evenly divided.

We did two runs at Stratford. They were about to launch their first junior parkrun event, so we ran the proposed course, mainly on grass. After a short break of no more than 15 minutes, we then ran the official course: three laps, a mix of grass and tarmac, and, by the final lap, my legs were really beginning to feel it.

Just one more parkrun to go and this was always an emotional moment as we returned to our home ground of Arrow Valley Park. The coach dropped us off at the outer reaches of the park, and sped away for the last time. Not everybody on the coach had taken part in the running. Several were volunteers who had marshalled, time-kept, recorded our individual performances and, of course, kept us fed and watered throughout a long, tough day. Others had run just selected routes but we all marched together, as a team, the few hundred yards to the start point of the final run in the fast-fading evening light.

As in previous years, the route was lined with dozens of people who had come out to welcome us back and applaud us in. High fives, hugs – my eyes were moist with the reaction we were getting. And then we were off for the final time, joined by local parkrunners who hadn't been able to take part in the rest of the day but were eager to be part of the finale. As we drifted across the finish line, by now in full darkness, our times were once again recorded and, for those who had run the full distance, a commemorative medal was presented.

That final leg was my slowest, but I had covered the full marathon distance in a day, and that was a real boost to my confidence in my preparations for the upcoming marathon in Venice. And that wasn't even an end to my running that weekend. Immediately after finishing, I drove the one hour or so up to Chris in Telford in readiness for a 10km race on the airfield of RAF Shawbury the following morning and, yes, I managed to complete that in a respectable time as well.

* * *

As much as my preparation for Venice seemed to be on track, this was not the case for Chris. He was fast approaching the end of his 22-year period of service with the RAF Regiment, and the uncertainty of what lay ahead was really beginning to play on his mind. How quickly had that time passed, for me at least? The memory of the tears rolling down my cheeks as I dropped my boy off at RAF Halton for his basic training certainly didn't seem over two decades old. Yet in that period he had served in conflict zones around the world, witnessed things that no one would ever wish to see, lost some close colleagues and been in some terrifying personal situations himself. The excellence of his service had been recognised on several occasions, most notably with an award in the Queen's birthday honours list. As his dad, I will always be immensely proud.

But now the future for Chris was hazy. Struggling to fit resettlement courses in to his busy full-time job, with a mortgage to pay which limited his ability to retrain for other occupations for which he would have been eminently suitable, the pressure on his time was mounting and something had to give. Sadly, it was his marathon training and shortly after the 10km race at RAF Shawbury, Chris announced that he simply wasn't ready to run the full marathon that was now only a few weeks away.

All was not lost. Chris managed to transfer his entry to the 10km race in Venice, so with flights and hotel booked, the family trip could still go ahead; I would just have to face the marathon by myself although, as in Rome, we probably wouldn't have run it together anyway.

But the bad luck didn't end there. The weekend after my parkrun marathon and the Shawbury 10km, I ran a half-marathon in Worcester. All was going swimmingly until, with less than half a mile to go, I felt a sharp, sudden pain in my left calf. It was one of those injuries where you just know it's best to stop. Sometimes you can feel a niggle coming on but keep going in the hope of running it off, but this was a 'stop now' moment. I massaged the area, and tried to stretch the calf gently, but the damage was done. Of course, with only a few hundred yards to go, I wasn't going to go home without my finishers' medal so I jogged, hobbled and walked to the finish line and set off home to get some ice on it.

My physio confirmed that I had torn a few fibres in my calf muscle. It was not a bad tear and there was hope that it could heal before the marathon. Of course, complete rest for at least two weeks was in order which was not what I had in mind at this stage of my training plan. I rested and I diligently repeated, on a daily basis, the strengthening exercises I had been shown. After two weeks I tried a little very gentle jogging. All seemed good. Speed was not a factor for me anyway for this marathon; my one and only goal was to cross the finish line and tick the box of having completed a marathon in my eighth decade. With three weeks to go, I gingerly completed a local 10km race. Again, no reaction from the calf but a little soreness from the right hamstring, probably due to my favouring that leg to protect the suspect calf.

Two weeks to go and now the real test. Would the calf stand up to longer mileage? I enlisted the help of my two favourite running buddies, Julie and Phillipa: you will have come across them both if you have read the previous books. The plan was a 15-mile out-and-back run with Julie, with Phillipa joining us for the final few miles. For nine miles it was an enjoyable chatty run at a non-demanding pace but then the calf pain gradually returned. Not the sharp pain I had felt in Worcester, but one that wasn't going to go away. I tried to run through it but the game was up. My dream of the Venice Marathon was gone. Rather than joining us for the final few miles, Phillipa became our rescue vehicle and returned a very disconsolate Doug to his home.

Even the prospect of possibly joining Chris running the Venice 10km run was denied me; the race was full by the time I applied. My only option was to carry my marathon entry over to the following year, 2019, and hope for better luck on the injury front.

* * *

The family trip to Venice with Chris, Lynne and Cam went ahead and was indeed memorable, although not for the reasons we envisaged when we booked it. On the day of the races, and particularly the day afterwards, we were awoken in the morning by the four rising tones of the *aqua alta* alarm siren, indicating the highest level alert for potential flooding. Venice was awash with one of the highest tides on record. Even the raised walkways that the local authorities quickly erected provided little protection as the water swept in, and the iconic St Mark's Square was soon under several feel of water. Never missing an opportunity to extract more euros from the tourist visitors, almost all the city's retailers suddenly produced stocks of elasticated-topped, plastic wading boots to offer at least some protection against the rising waters. The first pair I bought were not quite fit for purpose. Wading through the streets with Cam, for whom this was an extraordinary adventure that would forever stay in their memory, I was acutely aware that my left foot was significantly colder than my right one; it might only have been a pinhole leak but the water had soon found its way in.

It was also remarkable how quickly local shopkeepers adapted to what, for many, could have been a disastrous situation; they moved stock to higher shelves but basically continued as normal. Electric sockets were placed higher on the wall than we are used to at home – someone had thought that one through!

On the Sunday evening, not being able to travel too far from our hotel, we were lucky enough to find a table at a busy local restaurant. As we ate our meal, water was swirling around our feet and the waiters waded up and down the aisles – it was business as usual. Outside, rain was falling to add to the hardship. Unable or unwilling to drag their wheeled luggage through the flooded streets, bedraggled tourists struggled to carry their suitcases in their arms, or even balanced on their head, as they made their way to and from their hotels. Venice certainly has its charms but offers many challenges as well.

* * *

We had signed up to Venice to run a marathon, and while that didn't happen for either Chris or myself, that doesn't mean that no running took place. Chris did run the Venice 10km race but he wasn't overly impressed. Starting on the mainland in San Giuliano Park in the Venetian borough of Mestre, the route very quickly took the competitors on to the Liberty Bridge, the near two-and-a-half-mile-long structure that links the mainland to the lagoon islands of the city. The route was narrow and with the majority of participants being local people, many wanting to walk rather than run, they eagerly congregated towards the front at the start line. Of course, it was perfectly acceptable to walk the route but this left the runners who started further back having to weave around walkers, sometimes up to a dozen abreast, with many wielding walking poles.

Once off the bridge, and running through the docklands, it was much easier to maintain a steady pace and, as Chris neared the city, the crowd support grew. However, so did the depth of water his feet were now running through and, for the vast majority of people who took part in Venice in 2018, whether the 10km or the marathon, the overriding memory will be splashing through calf-deep water in the final stages.

There was, however, one running highlight of the trip for both Chris and I. Readers of my earlier books will know that I am a bit of a parkrun addict and, if I was ever to find myself in foreign parts on a Saturday morning, the first thing I would do was to see if there was a nearby parkrun. Farfalle parkrun was not exactly nearby; it was held in the city of Padua, some 25 miles west of Venice. Four of my running friends from my home Arrow Valley parkrun were also in Italy for the Venice races. They were all staying on the mainland in Mestre, so the journey was a little shorter for them.

At far too early an hour, Chris and I crept out of our room, leaving Lynne and Cam asleep, and made our way on foot to the nearby river bus terminal, where we caught the very first boat of the morning to the railway station. We boarded the train to Padua; the first stop was Mestre, where our friends Huw, Jayne, Andrew and Bridget were staying and linked up with us. Less than half an hour later we were at Padua station, but still had to find our way to Farfalle Park, *farfalle* being the Italian word for butterfly. From their website it seemed rather too far to walk in the time we had available, and the bus route that had been suggested didn't seem to have a stop outside the station. We commandeered a couple of taxis and, with over 30 minutes to go, we arrived at our destination, a lone parkrun teardrop flag giving us some confidence we were in the right place.

There were very few people around but eventually, the event director, Alessandro, came and introduced himself to us and gave us a hearty welcome. Minutes ticked by and still there seemed to be very few people who looked remotely dressed for running. At the very last minute, a few more cars arrived in the tiny car park. Numbers were swelled a little by a few other visitors who had signed up for the races in Venice, and had made the effort to get to Padua for a parkrun and, after Alessandro gave a briefing in Italian, one of his colleagues kindly delivered the same in English. Alessandro was positively jumping for joy at the size of the turnout, boosted by its foreign visitors and, as it turned out, this was indeed a record attendance for Farfalle parkrun, reaching the dizzying heights of 37!

After a celebratory start-line photo, we were set on our way to run four twisty laps of the park – very flat but with a variety of grass, trail, woodland and loose stony path. It was a run to enjoy, and I was lapped twice by the leader as I ran the first three laps with Chris, who then stretched his legs a little bit before his 10km race, and left me for dust on the final lap. A handful of marshals seemed to pop up at various places on the route to guide us on our way and Alessandro himself acted as race photographer, capturing us out on the route as well as at the finish line.

Having scanned our barcodes and finish tokens, this tiny band of yellow-vested volunteers then set about becoming baristas, opening up the tiny cafe at the park and offering a generous selection of hot drinks, cakes and pastries. Once we'd had our fill, they then phoned for a couple of taxis to take us all back to the railway station. An absolutely unique and heart-warming parkrun experience.

And there was one more cherry to put on to the top of the cake. When our results were posted, I had finished 27th out of the 37 runners. Not surprisingly, I was first in my age category, being the only over-70 present but, much to my astonishment, my time of a little over 29 minutes was the fastest ever recorded at Farfalle parkrun for my age group, this being the 34th running of the event! Yes, in my own mind I was the holder of a European running record and I may have mentioned it once or twice to Chris, and maybe a few other people as well!

Chapter 2

Turbulent waters

WITH MY septuagenarian marathon challenge delayed for a further year, it was time to set some more new goals. Yes, the equator target was still there but that was a good two or three years away, and I needed more immediate ambitions to keep the motivation up. I felt it was also time to think about a new charity to fundraise for. I had asked my friends to sponsor me on my foreign adventure runs to support the Midlands Air Ambulance Charity for several years. Indeed, the proceeds for my regular running talks, most of which take place in the Midlands region, would continue to go to this life-saving charity which receives no government support.

For upcoming overseas adventures, however, I now turned to support International Animal Rescue, a wonderful charity for which my daughter Angela works. On many of my running adventures overseas, I have had some amazing encounters with animals in their natural environments. Maybe the elephants in South Africa got a little too close for comfort, but then I was in their territory and I wouldn't be too happy if an elephant came into my home either!

I have become increasingly aware of the problems many species face, whether from man's cruel practices or destruction and contamination of their environments by the way we live our lives. This was brought home to me emphatically on my recent visit to Antarctica when a group of us in small rubber inflatables came across two giant humpback whales who were within touching distance of us. They entertained us for 15 minutes and could not have been more gentle, even though they possessed the power to cast us into the icy water. We don't own this planet; we share it with some magnificent species, and so, for the sake of future generations, I wanted to do something that would stop making life difficult for them. This charity not only rescues animals from suffering, but also rehabilitates and releases them back into the wild, while working to protect their natural habitats.

And so to a new challenge. With no more continents to chase on this planet, I turned my attention to running on islands. My trip to Easter Island had already been booked, and the city of Venice, which would hopefully host my full marathon (take two) was built on lagoon islands. Back in 2016 I had really enjoyed the challenge of four tough races in four days on the island of Cyprus, and one of my parkrun buddies, Paul, had expressed his wish to join me if I ever went back. This event was a joint collaboration between Arena Sports in Cyprus and 2:09 Events, the

British running travel company led by Mike Gratton, a former London Marathon winner.

Then another temptation was dangled in front of me. The Cyprus event had been such an outstanding success over many years that, in 2018, Mike had run a small test event on São Miguel Island in the Azores. This too had worked well with the same four-day, four-race format, so was also added to the 2:09 Events calendar for 2019. So there was the challenge I was looking for laid out in front of me: a half-marathon on Easter Island in May, four races in the Azores in September, the Venice Marathon in October, and four more races in Cyprus in November. Four islands, ten races, 100 miles in total. It was a tough but achievable plan, with a particularly busy autumn period, and before I had any change of heart the trips were all booked.

* * *

I was not the only one in the family to be setting new running challenges. Chris had entered the Sierra Leone Marathon in aid of the charity Streetchild, which helped children in that poorest of countries into education. For Chris, this was a deeply personal return visit. Back in 2000, as a member of 2 Squadron of the RAF Regiment, he had parachuted into that country, at the height of its civil war, as part of the British operation to evacuate foreign nationals and to help establish order. I had even been able to watch my own son descend into the jungle on the national evening news on television. Chris endured some terrifying moments during his time over there but returned safely to home shores with a deep affection for the country, its beautifully scenic beaches and jungles, and particularly, its poverty-stricken people. He wanted to give something back and this was his opportunity to do so.

Chris had also decided that he wouldn't be entering the Venice Marathon again, having transferred his previous year's entry over to the 10km race which, as I have alluded to earlier, he wasn't overly impressed with. For a very brief period this left me with the prospect of a solo trip to Venice to run my over-70 marathon, which I had vowed to do, but all was not lost. One of my running friends, Mike, was due to celebrate a significant birthday milestone on Christmas Eve of 2018, and his wife Michelle had organised a party in a local hall a couple of days before. Michelle had bought Mike a surprise present – entry into the 2019 Venice Marathon! Now, I know that any non-runners reading this would recoil at the fact that anyone would be delighted with getting a marathon entry as a birthday present, but we runners are a strange breed. The plan was to present Mike with his entry at his party, but secretly, Michelle had been using the power of social media to see if any of his friends would like to join them in Venice to run the marathon, the 10km, or just to party. The response was terrific. I, of course, was already in, and my run buddy Julie agreed to join me for the marathon. Over a dozen others also agreed; we even had 'Team Venice' T-shirts printed which we discreetly hid as we arrived at the party, and when the time came for the big reveal, we donned them and stood with Mike and Michelle for a group photo. Venice 2019 was going to be great.

* * *

For me at least, 2019 opened in the same way as 2018 had, with the Run Every Day January challenge for the mental health charity Mind. Once again, I set myself the target of running at least 5km each day and, although I finished about ten miles short of my 2018 total I still topped 150 miles for the month, which was a good training base for the upcoming trip to Easter Island at the end of May. I also celebrated my 300th parkrun at the beginning of February and, by an amazing coincidence, as I reached out for my finishing token after I had crossed the line and glanced down, I saw that my finishing position was 300th! Some things are meant to be.

For Chris, however, 2019 would prove to be his *annus horribilis*, and that is putting it mildly. I have already alluded to how the impending end of his full-time RAF career had led to anxiety and this, in turn, to social withdrawal which was so out of keeping with his usual personality. I fondly remembered the days when, with his friend Kim, they had persuaded their local town council to provide the necessary funds to launch what was then the very first parkrun in Shropshire. Telford parkrun had continued to go from strength to strength since.

There was more promising news for Chris on the job front when, in January, he was successfully interviewed for a training post with 605 Squadron of the RAF Reserves at nearby RAF Cosford. This at least meant that the prospect of having to move house in search of new employment had retreated. The brief optimism that this news brought was crushed a few days later, however, with the sad news that his wife Lynne had decided that she needed some space and time on her own, and would be leaving the family home although she would live nearby. Cam would remain at the family home with Chris and their pets, and Lynne and Chris were quickly able to agree on co-parenting matters to minimise the effect this would have on them. From the wider family circle, these situations are always sad and complex but there really is no other choice than to respect the decisions that had been made and to try and support the family as best we could. For Chris, however, it was a devastating blow to his already very fragile self-belief, and, if he thought life could get no more challenging, he was about to learn otherwise.

* * *

Both Chris and I were due to be out of the country at the same time towards the end of May on our respective new running adventures in Sierra Leone and on Easter Island. My own training was pretty much on track; after the heavy miles of January, I completed a half-marathon at Hampton Court Palace in London in March, and then the same distance in Stratford-upon-Avon a month later. Happily there was no recurrence of the calf problems that had blighted my preparations for Venice the year before.

For Chris, still adjusting to his new domestic circumstances and having less spare time to train, the journey towards marathon fitness was again becoming more difficult. Nevertheless, on the very same day that I was running around King Henry VIII's former stamping ground, Chris lined up at the start line of the Stafford half-marathon. He finished in a very creditable time of just below two hours, almost 20 minutes quicker than my time in London but, in the final stages of his race, he began to suffer from an extremely painful headache. This rang alarm bells.

Some years previously, Chris had encountered a few similar episodes, relatively short-lasting, and with considerable time periods of many months between each bout. The pain had been excruciating. Medical consultations had led to the prescription of strong painkillers but even these seemed to have little effect. At that time I was still working at the University of Birmingham's Medical School and had just finished editing a textbook on neurological and psychiatric disorders, written by specialists within their field. This included a chapter on headache disorders, and raised the possibility that Chris may have been suffering from a rare condition called cluster headache, named because it was commonly episodic, occurring in clusters, with sometimes remission periods of years in between. Indeed, Chris was eventually given this diagnosis.

Somewhat surprisingly, although admittedly it is a rare condition, cluster headache is not readily known about or understood, even among some members of the medical profession. Perhaps the most stark reminder of its effect on its sufferers is the alternative nomenclature, 'suicide headaches'. Many people in the past have sadly taken their own lives, unable to tolerate the unrelenting pain.

Chris's past experiences with this debilitating condition had been relatively short-lived but on this occasion, that headache towards the end of his half-marathon was just the beginning of an acute episode that would last for eight or nine weeks, but would have lasting consequences far beyond that. As the separate attacks became more intense and more frequent, often up to ten times in any 24-hour period with no lessening during the night, Chris was eventually able to get a prescription for a home oxygen supply; breathing pure oxygen through a face mask was one of the few interventions that could reduce the length and intensity of an episode. However, even that would not work every time and eventually he was shown how to self-administer another drug, sumatriptan, by injection into his abdomen or thigh. Only three injections of sumatriptan could be given in any 24-hour period, so they really were to be used as a last resort.

I have never suffered from a cluster headache myself, so it would be pointless for me to try and articulate what it must be like. Once Chris had reached the stage of having to use sumatriptan he was asked to keep a diary:

time of onset, duration of episode, what interventions were required to terminate it, and a pain score on a scale of one to ten (the Kip scale, named after Bob Kipple, an American who had been a long-term sufferer). For example, a score of four would indicate 'Starting to get bad, want to be left alone'; a score of seven would be 'Wake up, sleep not an option, take the beast for a walk and finally fall into bed exhausted' and a ten would be 'Major pain, screaming, head banging, A&E trip. Depressed. Suicidal.'

Just as an insight into what Chris was going through, these are two extracts from his diary, included with his permission, of course.

At 2.45pm one day in mid-April, he wrote, 'Severe CH came on suddenly, following a bath. Used oxygen for 20 minutes and no sign of relief, so used sumatriptan jab too. After jab, approximately 12 minutes until relief, although it does feel a little like it's still there a bit.' Just four hours later came, 'Most severe CH yet. Came on suddenly and was straight on the oxygen. Used oxygen for 20 minutes and no improvement. Shortly after, I remember feeling light-headed and the next thing, I was on the sofa. I panicked as it appeared that I had blacked out. I called my wife to come and look after Cam, then dialled 999. The ambulance took around ten minutes. I have never felt pain like this in all my life. The paramedics arrived and started their observations, while I continued on oxygen. I was then taken to A&E by ambulance.' On both occasions he recorded Kip scores of ten.

In a great deal of distress, Chris had managed to phone me before the ambulance arrived and I raced up to the A&E in Telford to sit with him until investigations were complete. By the time I arrived, yet another episode had subsided and I was eventually able to drive him back home and stay until the following morning, by which time he had had three further episodes during the night, two scoring seven and one scoring nine.

The attacks continued in unrelenting fashion, up to a dozen times a day, for at least another week until he was finally able to attend a specialist clinic in Birmingham for severe headache disorders. Having received confirmation that cluster headache was indeed the correct diagnosis, Chris was given an injection of a local anaesthetic into the greater occipital nerve in the back of his head and, over a period of several days, the intensity and frequency of the attacks gradually diminished. He still suffered from shadow attacks, which he described as a feeling that something was going on inside his brain, but without the severe pain, and this has persisted for over a year now although, thankfully, the severe attacks have largely remained at bay.

One thing was certain, and this was a decision taken out of his hands by his medical advisers; the Sierra Leone Marathon would have to be put on to the back burner, for the current year at the very least. However, all was not lost on the fundraising front for Street Child. Chris had devised a virtual run, with a medal in the shape of the country of Sierra Leone. All proceeds from the entry fees went to the charity, and to qualify for the medal you had to run a distance of nine miles, this being the average distance a child in Sierra Leone had to walk each day to get to school, and that was the lucky ones who had a school place. He had quite a few takers in Telford where he lived and I decided to help out by trying to see if I could get some of the Redditch running community involved.

I have a running route of exactly nine miles that starts and finishes at my house. What made it more appealing was that when the route was plotted on Strava, the social fitness network that tracks your running routes using satellite data, the shape of a matchstick dog appeared, complete with head, body, legs and tail. For the uninitiated, we runners call this Strava art! To make the run even more appealing to many, I offered everyone who finished a celebratory glass of wine at my home to accompany their medal presentation. It went down well and, during the early weeks of May, I led no fewer than three matchstick dog runs with many of my local friends. To make the first one even more special, Chris had recovered sufficiently to make the one-hour drive down from Telford to present the medals himself. He was, of course, accompanied by an oxygen supply and his auto-injectors just in case.

* * *

Although Chris would no longer be visiting Sierra Leone, my trip to the half-marathon on Easter Island was now fast approaching. I was thankful for the recent improvement in Chris's condition as this made it easier for me to be far from home and, thankfully, in contrast to when I had visited Antarctica and Angela, my daughter, was ill at home, I would still have access to the internet to keep in touch. The matchstick dog runs and the two half-marathons I had recently completed meant I was in pretty good shape to take on the challenge, even if my performances were beginning to decline year by year. The important thing was that I was still enjoying my running.

There was a bit of a curveball thrown at us just four days before departure when all the entrants from Marathon Tours were sent an email informing us that information had been received from the race director of an outbreak of dengue fever on Easter Island. The races would still go ahead as planned, but we were given the option of postponing our entry to the 2020 event. I spoke to Clare, who I would be travelling with, and also sought advice from a running friend of mine who was a senior member of the healthcare team at my GP surgery. Dengue fever is a mosquito-borne disease which causes a flu-like illness and both Clare and I had already packed plenty of insect repellent and long-sleeved garments as you would when visiting any tropical island. We decided to go ahead with the trip and informed Marathon Tours. It would seem that everybody else making the journey came to the same decision.

* * *

The big day arrived and for once, my pre-trip anxiety had not been too bad. Possibly my preoccupation with

Chris's health had been a distraction, and also, for the first time, I was now sharing the whole experience with Clare. With increasing age comes increasing forgetfulness, for me at any rate, so I was constantly checking and double-checking my packing list to make sure that nothing crucial had been left behind. I was also mindful of how my anxiety sometimes makes me feel very rushed during the airport check-in and security procedures, and didn't want to repeat my Antarctica experience where I had managed to leave a whole folder of important documents at check-in, not realising until I had passed through security! At least I had another pair of eyes looking out for me this time.

Our journey began with an early evening flight to Paris from our nearest airport in Birmingham, a short but boisterous journey with many of the passengers being families on their way to Disneyland Paris for the half-term break. Next came the overnight flight to Santiago in Chile: 13 hours in a somewhat more tranquil environment. A distinctly average meal was accompanied by some much-needed complimentary wine and cognac, clearly offered to help us sleep. The lights were dimmed and for the next eight or nine hours or so I twisted and turned in my seat in an effort to get a few hours of catnapping in.

Part way through the night came a moment of panic. I had managed to doze off with both of my hearing aids in. In a brief moment of wakefulness I reached to my left ear, only to find nothing in place. Oh dear, a potentially expensive error. I rummaged around on my seat, under the blanket, on the floor, trying hard not to wake Clare, asleep in the seat beside me, but there was no sign of it. My tired mind just imagined the worst scenario of the crunching sound it would make as somebody accidentally stepped on it, but, as is so often the case when you fear the worst, a much more positive outcome emerged. As the cabin lights came back on to signal preparations for breakfast, the lady in the seat behind spotted the missing device on the floor in front of her and handed it back to me. Lesson learned: don't wear hearing aids on long-haul flights.

* * *

We arrived at our hotel mid-morning in Santiago after a surprisingly inexpensive taxi ride from the airport. The reception staff advised us that our room wasn't yet ready but, on payment of an additional fee of $70, another room could be found for us. We declined their kind offer and waited in the foyer to people-watch as other guests arrived, hoping to spot a few visitors, usually by their footwear, who might look like runners. Magically, after only 30 minutes of waiting, our allotted room was now ready and our decision not to spend the extra $70 was fully vindicated.

Our itinerary included a visit to a local winery that afternoon but, with a couple of hours to spare, Clare and I had a quick freshen up before setting off to explore the local neighbourhood around the hotel. Our primary goal was to find somewhere to run the following day: we were only going to be in Santiago for a couple of days but it would have been rude not to enjoy at least one run in the capital city of Chile.

Nearby was a large shopping mall, which we briefly investigated, and beyond that was the Parque Araucano, a passing inspection of which meant we had discovered our primary goal for the following day's run. We had crossed many time zones to find this park but we were also now more than 2,300 miles south of the equator. That meant that, in the space of a single day, we had been transported from late spring to deepest autumn. I really found this quite hard to come to terms with as my feet scrunched through large piles of fallen leaves.

There was one of those brief moments of hilarity as we made our way back to the hotel. Just outside the shopping mall was a Starbucks and we decided that we had enough time for a quick cup of invigorating coffee. Of course, this coffee house chain likes to write your name on the takeaway cup that it serves its coffee in.

'What is your name?' asked the young lady who took my order, although her accent made clear that English was not her first language.

'Doug,' I replied.

'How do you spell that?' she smiled.

'D-O-U-G.'

I paid and waited for my drink. When it came, the cup was labelled 'Enjoy, Touk'! As we sat outside, I took a photo of the cup and shared it on Facebook. For quite some time after that, I would have to live with the name of Touk.

* * *

An hour or so later, we were waiting in the hotel lobby for our first excursion of the trip, to a local winery. Now was our chance to meet the people we would be sharing our journey with. First and foremost was Jacqui, our Marathon Tours representative, who would be leading not only the Easter Island leg of the trip but also the extension to Peru. Jacqui was an experienced tour leader for the company, having led several previous visits to Easter Island, but I doubt at that moment that she realised quite what a challenging time lay ahead of her.

I also recognised a couple of familiar faces, Kathy and Megan, who had sailed on the *Ioffe* with me on the previous year's trip to Antarctica, and then I was introduced to four other American ladies, Catharine, Liz, Kate and Jenny, who had also run the 2018 Antarctica half-marathon, but had been on the sister ship, the *Vavilov*, and so ran 24 hours after we did. It was quite an Antarctic reunion.

It was about an hour's coach journey from Santiago out to the renowned Concha y Toro winery in the Maipo Valley, passing through the much poorer suburbs of the city and into some spectacular mountainous scenery. Our Chilean guide gave us an informative discourse on the current geographic, economic and political status of the country, almost with an air of humility in his voice. Chile really is a unique country in terms of its shape, being almost 2,700 miles in length from north to south, but only 217 miles from west to east at its very widest point. This gave it a unique range of environments and climates, ranging from the heat of the Atacama Desert in the northern regions to the chilling ferocity of the Drake Passage off the southernmost tip.

The winery did not disappoint; it was surrounded by mountains, with a lake reflecting the autumn colours of the surrounding trees, a garden housing over two dozen varieties of wine grapes and a vineyard stretching away from the spectacular summer residence of the original owners, who founded the winery in 1883. We examined equipment used for wine production in bygone days, explored the depths of the extensive wine cellars and, of course, sampled three different styles of the finished product; it would have been rude not to.

Once back at the hotel, it was then time to attend the formal welcome meeting with Jacqui, to pick up some updated information about what lay ahead, and to get to know our fellow travellers a little better. Clare and I had planned to stay for a short while before going out for a meal in the city, but the hotel had laid on a great buffet meal, the wine and cocktails flowed freely, and the conversation was excellent. In particular the opportunity to compare notes with our new American friends, who had experienced the very same Antarctica the previous year as I had done, but with a 24-hour time difference between us, was fascinating. Only twice during that time would we have been together; at the welcome briefing in Buenos Aires and then again on the decks of *Ioffe* for the celebratory post-race barbecue but, of course, we didn't know each other then.

With an early start the following morning for our final full day on mainland Chile, Clare and I abandoned the idea of a meal and made our way, slightly unsteadily, to get a good night's sleep. It had been a really uplifting day.

* * *

Valparaíso. We only had a couple of hours to explore, but what a crazy, chaotic and colourful city; Chile's major sea port and the home of the Chilean Navy. Near the waterfront stood the imposing building of the naval headquarters and a spectacular monument commemorating the Battle of Iquique of 1879 when Chile was pitted against Bolivia and Peru. The inland backdrop to this was hills, hills and more hills, many so steep that it would have been impossible for a motor vehicle to navigate them safely. Linked by winding alleyways and uneven staircases, the safest way to venture along the perilously steep streets, unless you were truly fit and able, was to use the aged *ascensores*, wooden funicular lifts with the two counterbalanced cabins hauling each other up and down the steep rail. Around the houses, electric and communication cables were all above ground, a wild, spaghetti-like tangle attached to wooden poles at regular intervals with occasional workmen hanging in a sling off them, trying to decipher which wire was which. But it was the colour that enveloped you that was really striking. Houses and cabins, some of them wooden, lined the precipitous streets and were painted in every shade imaginable.

Many of them were in plain, pastel colours, but other buildings were entirely covered in the most amazing street art, cartoon figures and colourful murals. One wall was emblazoned with the motto, 'WE ARE NOT HIPPIES: WE ARE HAPPIES'.

Our next stop was the adjacent resort city of Viña del Mar, and the contrast in character to Valparaíso could not have been more striking; it is a modern, tourist-focused city of hotels and restaurants with wide roads lined with palm trees. It was there that we stopped for a very pleasant lunch, and the opportunity to make another new friend.

Drew sat opposite Clare and I and introduced himself. He was a New Yorker, a senior executive of a large multimedia company with many of the world's top magazine titles within its portfolio. Above all, Drew was clearly a true gentleman. If you had passed him in the street, you would not immediately identify this tall and sturdily built figure as a marathon runner, but that was exactly what he was. Not the fastest by any means, but what he lacked in speed he more than made up for with sheer determination. For Drew, Easter Island would be the South American leg of his Seven Continents Challenge at the full marathon distance. He had already completed the marathon in Antarctica back in 2013, but the continents weren't his only marathon goal. He was also aiming for the target of the full distance in each of the 50 US states, and now had only a handful of them to go.

After the meal, the three of us took a stroll together along the beach, largely deserted as the holiday season was now rapidly drawing to a close. On returning to our coach for the journey back to Santiago, a rather glum-faced Jacqui boarded and said she had some important announcements to make. I had been seated next to Jacqui during the meal but she had been constantly getting up and down to make or receive phone calls, and had hardly been able to eat any of her food; the busy life of a tour leader, or so I thought. Now we were about to discover what the problem was. Was it related to the dengue fever scare?

First, the good news; the race was still going ahead, BUT the five-star luxury accommodation at the Hanga Roa Hotel on Easter Island, which had been promised and paid for, and indeed had been used by Marathon Tours on all their previous visits to the island, was no longer available to us, with no explanation as to why. Jacqui went on to explain that alternative accommodation was being found for us, but that it would not be of the same quality; the group was likely to be split across more than one hotel and that it was doubtful we would have access to wifi.

The reaction to this news was mixed. From my personal point of view, I would never decide to enter an overseas running adventure on the basis of the hotel accommodation on offer as part of the package. In fact, for many of my previous running adventures, my overnight lodging would have struggled to get into the one-star category. All I wanted was a bed, some clean sheets and a pillow to rest my head and, happily, Clare was of the same opinion. Jacqui had said we would receive compensation at a later date. Whatever had gone wrong, we could do nothing about it; nor, indeed, could Jacqui. I felt quite sorry for her. She was the sole representative of Marathon Tours out there and had some fairly unhappy customers on her hands, and an already challenging job had now been made much more difficult.

Some of the party were soon on their phones, booking their own hotels on Easter Island. Indeed, some were able to pick up the few remaining rooms at the Hanga Roa Hotel, but the vast majority of us were happy to go along with whatever could be arranged. The show must go on.

* * *

On our return to Santiago, there was finally a brief window of opportunity to enjoy a short run on Chilean soil. Clare and I set off from our hotel, walking through the shopping mall so as not to alert any security guards, and then picked up the pace again as we entered the Parque Araucano. It was a cool autumn evening; we ran footpaths and trails, among palm trees, rose gardens and giant carved wooden statues. We crossed the footbridge into the adjacent Parque Juan Pablo II, ran a lap around there, and then returned to our start point. Just three miles but, as ever, three miles in unfamiliar but scenic surroundings that lifted the spirits after the travel, the tight itinerary and the unexpected surprise revelations the day had delivered.

We grabbed a quick bite to eat in the shopping mall on the way back and then it was time for an early night.

Ahead of us lay a 2.30am alarm call, before the final leg of our journey, around 2,400 miles across the vast expanses of the South Pacific Ocean, to the magic of Easter Island.

Chapter 3

A band of brothers

WEDNESDAY, 29 May 2019 – the day I would finally set foot on Easter Island and, by coincidence, my 71st birthday. After our early morning wake-up call, we had all made it through to the departure lounge at Santiago International Airport in plenty of time for our 6.30am take-off slot. The only problem was that no aircraft was available to take us! So far, this trip was not going smoothly.

We did finally get airborne, but almost five hours later than scheduled, and were now heading for what is a tiny speck in a vast ocean. For our in-flight meal, and to compensate us for the delay, we were offered a choice of coffee, tea, beer or wine. The day was still young but I opted for the latter, and managed two rather substantial glasses of a very pleasant Chilean red – it was my birthday, after all.

So, after all the months of planning, I was finally heading for one of the most mysterious islands on the planet, less than a third of the area of the Isle of Wight.

For my international readers, this is a small island off the south coast of England. As with any notable destination that I visit to run, I had done quite a bit of reading beforehand to try and prepare myself for what I was going to experience. There were so many unanswered questions, and even the experts couldn't agree among themselves. There simply aren't any written historical records. Who were the original settlers on this tiny speck of an island, thousands of miles from the nearest mainland? The island is famous for its moai, a series of huge monolithic human structures carved from rock. When had they been made, how had they been moved and, perhaps most importantly, what did they represent?

For what it is worth, this is the potted history of Easter Island that had been planted in my mind before I set foot there. Sometime between 800 and 1200 the very first settlers had arrived, but where had they sailed from? The general consensus of opinion was that the original inhabitants came from the Polynesian islands to the west. Indeed, many of the historical relics to be found on the island are very typical of Polynesian culture. But, hang on a minute; no greater authority than Thor Heyerdahl, the renowned Norwegian explorer, argued that the original settlers had come from Peru in South America to the east. He had led an archaeological expedition to the island in 1955, spending several months excavating many sites, and concluded that the Polynesians did not arrive until the mid-16th century, after which they drove the South Americans out. With general agreement that the moai date back to between 1250 and 1500, Heyerdahl argued that they were erected by the South Americans and not people of Polynesian origin. Whatever the history, and most experts have now dismissed Heyerdahl's theories, for around 1,000 years the islanders lived in almost complete isolation from the rest of the world.

And then, in 1722, a Dutch sailing ship drew into the shore for a 24-hour visit. It was Easter Sunday so the captain, Admiral Roggeveen, decided to name it Easter Island, although to the native inhabitants it will always be Rapa Nui, and to the Chileans, who now claim sovereignty over the island, it is Isla de Pascua. Roggeveen recorded that the natives were generally friendly, were largely fair-skinned Polynesians, although some had darker skins, and that they lived in long, low huts of reed, resembling upturned boat hulls, with well-cultivated fields and dense forests around them. One thing that really attracted his attention, though, was the numerous giant rock carvings that overlooked most of the coastline, the first sighting of the moai by European eyes.

Just over 50 years later, the renowned English explorer Captain James Cook sailed in during his second major voyage to the southern hemisphere, and picked up a supply of sweet potatoes for his scurvy-ridden crew from the natives, whom he described as Polynesian in appearance. During his brief visit, Captain Cook noted that, in contrast to Admiral Roggeveen's observations, cultivated areas were few and far between, that most of the forests had disappeared and many of the moai had been toppled.

In all likelihood, both of these visits occurred during a period which had seen huge upheaval on the island. Quite simply, the growing population had outgrown the limited resources on such a tiny, remote island. Forests were felled for the wood, fierce inter-tribal wars broke out and reports of widespread cannibalism were rife. With the moai spread around the island being seen as representations of tribal ancestors, one of the manifestations of these wars was the rather childish toppling of those worshipped by rival tribes.

Even worse was to follow in the second half of the 19th century. In 1862, Peruvian slave raiders captured around 1,500 men and women, about half of the population at the time, to work in Peruvian guano mines (guano was basically bird excrement, and valued as an agricultural fertiliser, but being deposited in very inaccessible locations such as sea or land caves and cliff faces made its extraction a dangerous business). The majority died in the brutal conditions and, after the Bishop of Tahiti forced the kidnappers to repatriate the small number who had survived, smallpox killed most of those who made the return sea journey, with the remainder bringing the disease to those left on the island. With passing whaling ships bringing tuberculosis as well, by the 1870s, the population of Easter Island had declined to around 100.

In the space of a devastating decade over 97 per cent of the island's population had died or been captured, and a wealth of Rapa Nui cultural knowledge was lost forever.

Chile annexed Easter Island in 1888 but showed little interest in developing it. The Rapa Nui people were confined to the only town of Hanga Roa and the remainder of the island was largely given over to sheep grazing. Until 1966, the island was managed by the Chilean Navy and the local people were exploited, poorly paid, not allowed to vote and had their language suppressed. They were then colonised, given Chilean citizenship, and interbreeding with immigrants has diluted further the islanders' own cultures. To this day there remains tension between those of Rapa Nui ancestry and the Chileans.

* * *

After five and a half hours of flying, I caught my first glimpse of the mysterious island as we descended towards the airport. I was quite surprised to see such a lush expanse of trees below us, but Mother Nature had had a few centuries to replenish the island's stocks after the deforestation reported by Captain Cook. The airport we were heading for had been built in 1967 and this had, of course, opened up Easter Island to tourism for the first time, although a lack of basic facilities such as water supply and electricity, not to mention a shortage of hotels on such a tiny island, meant that its capacity was very limited. The airfield did have one major claim to fame, though – it boasted the longest runway in the whole of South America.

This seemingly absurd feather in the cap arose from an extension to the existing airstrip, completed with funding from the United States in 1988, which allowed it to act as an emergency landing site for the Space Shuttle programme. It was never used as such.

As I walked down the steps of our aircraft into a pleasantly warm atmosphere, a few drops of rain started to fall. Within seconds the heavens opened. We had several hundred yards to walk to reach the terminal building, which would have qualified as little more than a cabin at any other airfield, but by the time we reached it we were all soaked to the skin. Welcome to Easter Island.

Having collected our baggage we were greeted by Hugo, who would be our guide on the island. A tall, muscular man, clearly with Polynesian blood in his ancestral background, Hugo also carried a few scars of some skirmishes in his younger years. Not only did he have an encyclopaedic knowledge of the history of the island and its artefacts, he would also prove to be a great judge of the best places for food and drink in Hanga Roa. After Hugo greeted us each individually by hanging a garland of deep red flowers around our necks, Jacqui explained that accommodation had been found for us, but that we would be split between two hotels, although they were very close to each other.

The whole group, minus the few who had managed to arrange a room at the Hanga Roa hotel resort, our originally intended destination, were bussed the relatively short distance from the airport to the O'tai hotel in the town. As we stood in the pleasant grounds, in warm sunshine, Jacqui read out a list of just over a dozen of us who would be housed at the Manavai hotel, just a couple of hundred yards up the road. This included Clare and myself, as well as two of our new American friends, Catharine and Liz.

My initial impression of the Manavai was that we had got the better deal. In contrast to the relatively modern buildings of the O'tai, our hotel looked exactly as I would expect to see on a tropical, South Pacific island: stunning gardens crammed with trees, colourful plants and wooden carvings, an elevated platform from which you could look out over the coastline, and a splendid swimming pool. The helpful hotel staff showed us to our rooms, and Clare and I were delighted to find Catharine and Liz housed next door.

But then things began to unravel. The hotel had clearly been closed for some weeks as this was the region's off-season. Whatever had gone wrong with our originally booked accommodation meant they had to hastily reopen to house unexpected guests. As Clare and I opened the door to our room, the atmosphere would best be described as musty; it had evidently been closed up for a few weeks, but nothing that a good airing and a few open windows wouldn't clear. The bedding was clean, the furnishings were pleasant enough, the bathroom was perfectly adequate and the little outside wooden patio had chairs and a hammock to relax on. We were quite satisfied, even though it didn't offer the luxury we had paid for.

Others who had been allocated to the Manavai weren't so lucky! Within an hour or two of settling in, suitcases were being repacked and wheeled back out to reception, with tales of bloodstains and insect droppings on bed sheets, and cockroaches scrambling across the floor. Even our neighbours, Catharine and Liz, were packing their bags and seeking room at the O'tai. While they were extremely close friends, and had travelled together extensively, even they weren't prepared to tolerate an en-suite bathroom with no door! The Manavai numbers were dwindling rapidly.

* * *

It was, of course, still my birthday. After a brief exploratory walk around those parts of Hanga Roa close to our hotel, Clare treated me to a local beer, and then we met up with the rest of the party for a meal at a local restaurant. Jacqui explained to us that there would be a full investigation into why our original hotel reservation, which had been fully paid for in advance, was then suddenly withdrawn at the last minute.

We would be compensated in due course, but in the meantime, as a gesture of goodwill, Marathon Tours would foot the bill for our meal. It was a fun evening; nothing much was going to plan, but we were all ready to make the most of whatever lay ahead. Once again, red wine appeared from nowhere and the restaurant even produced a tiny birthday cake with two candles on it for, as my birthday ended at midnight, so Clare's birthday began.

* * *

Although only a few of us remained at our hotel, the ever-helpful staff laid on a splendid buffet breakfast the following morning, and cooked us all omelettes, before we joined the rest of the group and set off on our very first excursion to the eastern end of the island.

There really was only one place to start our journey and that was at the quarry cut inside the huge volcanic crater of Rano Raruka; it was there that the moai were carved. Once we had disembarked from the bus, Hugo gave us a brief geological lesson, showing us various types of rock to be found in the area; some, like basalt, were hard enough to be used as a tool, and, most importantly, tuff or tufa, the softer, solidified volcanic ash from which the moai were cut. As we climbed the steep slopes and steps of the trail leading up to the quarry, we passed dozens of moai, some embedded in the steep grassy slopes, some fallen and broken. At the quarry site itself, unfinished moai could still be seen in situ; clearly something had happened suddenly that had driven the workers away, never to return. Trenches were cut either side at each new site and teams of workers would labour for months, chipping away at the tuff with basalt picks, with the facial features uppermost. Those who had drawn the short straw worked underneath the effigy, chiselling away at the spinal level, and archaeological evidence shows that many of these lost their lives when the weight of the carving fractured the fragile rock connection and brought the whole statue down on top of them. Once finally separated from the surrounding rock, the moai then had to be hauled upright, remembering that they could each weigh over 80 tons, and then transported down the steep grassy slopes of the crater, where the finer detail could be added. It was little wonder that we had seen so many fallen and broken moai on those slopes. It is hard to find words that satisfactorily express my feelings at what we learned at Rano Raruka.

From the heights of the volcanic crater, and looking down towards the coastline to the east, we could already see our next destination, Tongariki. That houses the largest *ahu* on the island, an *ahu* being the rock platform on which the moai were stood. During the civil wars on the island, the moai were toppled and the *ahu* swept out to sea. A tsunami washed the *ahu* back to the shore, however, and, in the late 20th century work began to restore this site. Now, no fewer than 15 moai stand aloft on this impressive structure, just one retaining the circular rock hat on its head, known as a *pukao*.

After visiting a re-created site which showed how the Rapa Nui villagers cultivated their crops in small, circular plots surrounded by protective rock walls, and which contained a reconstruction of the low 'upturned hull' reed huts noted by Admiral Roggeveen, we paused at a local restaurant for an authentic Rapa Nui chicken and rice lunch. Next stop was Te Pito Kura to witness *Paro*, not only the largest moai ever to be moved and lifted on to an *ahu*, but also one of the last to be toppled. Sadly, *Paro* still lies in pieces, with the brown-coloured *pukao*, which itself weighed 12 tons, lying on the grass nearby. How had these huge structures been moved from the quarry and then lifted on to their *ahu*? Rapa Nui tradition says that they walked to their final destination and that may not be as far-fetched as it sounds. It has been shown that by tying ropes around a concrete replica of a moai, a team of people can make it move forward on a flat surface by rocking it from side to side while pulling from the front, and restraining it at the rear. I'm not convinced there were too many flat surfaces around for the Rapa Nui workers, though. Maybe tree trunks could have been used as rollers, but when it comes to hauling the moai upright, and then lifting it up on to an *ahu*, I have yet to see a convincing explanation of that.

Nearby to where *Paro* lay was another of Easter Island's mysteries, a near-perfect spherical rock, half embedded in the ground. Known as 'The Navel of the World', it is said to emit spiritual power. Certainly, if you place a magnetic compass on top of it, the needle goes crazy and doesn't know which way to point, although the cynical scientist within me thinks that this is more likely to be magnetic elements within the rock itself rather than any mystical influences.

Our final call on this utterly unforgettable day of discovery was Anakena, the legendary landing site of the founding king of the Rapa Nui people, Hotu Matu'a. Among sandy beaches and palm trees, seven more moai stood aloft on their *ahu*, four complete with *pukao*, one without, and two others on which only the lower part of the body remained. Nearby, a single and very stocky moai was known locally as 'Mike Tyson'. Warning signs around the site alerted visitors to the dangers of branches and coconuts falling on your head, and of imprisonment if you were to cause any damage to any of the historical relics. And, of course, there was the attraction of the beach, one of very few sandy beaches on the island with the majority of the coastline dominated by towering cliffs and chaotic mounds of rock and boulders. The temptation to take our shoes and socks off and take a little paddle in the relatively warm waters of the Pacific Ocean was a little too much for most of us to resist.

* * *

It was still Clare's birthday so, on our return to the hotel, we joined up with Catharine, Liz and Drew for a celebration meal in the Mahalo restaurant, situated on the first floor of the Manavai, and which had been recommended as one of the finest on the island. It did not disappoint. After the meal, the next item on our unrelenting agenda was the official opening ceremony for the weekend's events. Apart from the marathon and half-marathon, there were also 5km and 10km road races, a triathlon and a mountain bike race around the island. It was while waiting for our group to gather after using the bathrooms that a moment of pure comedy gold happened.

There were, by now, only six of us remaining at the Manavai, after all the problems of dirty bedding, missing doors and unwanted creepy-crawlies in the rooms. Drew was trying to persuade Clare and I that we too should jump ship and move to the O'tai where most of the party were now based. We were insistent that we were quite happy where we were, and Clare uttered that immortal phrase, 'We are a band of brothers!' No sooner had those words left her lips than Jessica and Courtney, two of the remaining six, came past us, hauling their suitcases behind them. It could not have been more perfectly timed.

Their reason for leaving was a new one; since arriving they had been repeatedly disturbed by the loud noises of what I shall describe as adult activity from a nearby room, followed by fierce arguments. Enough was enough, and they too were now off to find alternative accommodation in the town. The band of brothers was now down to four. Our sole remaining comrades were a lovely couple from Portland, Oregon, Jim and Claire, who, fortuitously happened to occupy the cabin next door. Jim was a businessman and here to support runner Claire, who quickly became known as 'Claire with an i' to avoid any confusion. With a remarkable past history of endurance running, Claire had entered the full marathon in one of the more senior age categories; it would, of course, be inappropriate to reveal which one!

* * *

The opening ceremony was a truly surreal experience, and yet another demonstration that the relationship between the race organisers and our tour company was what you might describe as strained. We were bussed out to a large agricultural-looking building, inside which we could see many people seated in front of a stage. Our Marathon Tours group, and just our group among all the other competitors, were led however to a small, open-sided outbuilding and invited to stand around the perimeter where the race director, Rodrigo, welcomed us all to Easter Island and said a few words about what lay ahead. Our race packet pick-up would be at the pre-race pasta party, but there would now be a charge to attend that. Jacqui knew Rodrigo from previous years' visits to the marathon but the dialogue between them was a little frosty.

Once Rodrigo had left, a very scantily clad Rapa Nui warrior leapt into the small central arena. A tattoo across his shoulder, an ornate feathered headdress, and just two small, triangular pieces of fleecy cloth covered his nether regions, front and back. He performed an acrobatic ceremonial dance for us, interspersed with boisterous chanting; the tiny flaps covering his manhood were just about enough to maintain decency. He then produced a chicken carcass, which had been baked in a hole in the ground, and proceeded to move around each one of us, inviting us to take a piece of meat as a gesture of welcome. I made sure that my piece looked very well cooked. Then he disappeared into the darkness, and that was it; that was the opening ceremony, at least for our tour party.

* * *

On the following morning, our final sightseeing trip on this intriguing island took us first to Vinapu, on the southern coast. Once again, the tribal wars of the 18th and 19th centuries had seen the moai toppled, and their fragments and *pukao* lay scattered on the ground. Embedded up to the neck in the grass was the very weathered and barely recognisable head of a moai, and nearby stood the remains of a rare female version. However, the most perplexing part of this site was the two large *ahu* from which the moai had fallen. One, like the many we had seen the previous day, was a conglomeration of rocks and boulders that had been brought together to provide a flat-topped platform. In the other, however, the rocks, each weighing many tons, had been skilfully carved with great precision to fit together like a giant, three-dimensional jigsaw puzzle, with no mortar between them. This aesthetic perfection was very typical of the work of the Incas in Peru, and was one of the leading arguments put forward by Thor Heyerdahl for his theory that the original occupiers of Easter Island came from South America and not Polynesia.

There was just one more stop, Orongo, on the very south-western tip of the island. A stone village was situated on the edge of precipitous 300m cliffs to one side, and the huge crater of the dormant volcano, Rano Kau, on the other. Orongo was also the original home of the most exquisitely carved moai, *Hoa Hakananai'a*, which was removed by the Royal Navy in 1868 and now resides in the British Museum in London. Having visited the island, and seen how important these archaeological relics are to the islanders, this makes me sad and I, for one, would be very happy if we let *Hoa Hakananai'a* go back home.

Orongo was also the location for the ancient annual contest of the island's Birdman cult to choose the representative of the chief god, Makemake, from the young men of Rapa Nui. If you look out to sea from the top of the cliffs at Orongo you can see a sharp pinnacle of rock just a few hundred yards from the shoreline. About the same distance beyond that is a tiny rocky island, and a little further out a rather larger island, Moto Nui, its steep rocky coastline constantly battered by ferocious Pacific waves. It was on Moto Nui, and only this island, that the manutara bird, or sooty tern, would lay its eggs. On the given signal, the chosen contestants would first have to scale down the near vertical cliff-face of Orongo, swim out to Moto Nui, climb on to the island while being battered by the waves and then collect a manutara egg. They weren't finished yet! Having placed the egg in a little pouch attached to their foreheads, they then had to swim back to the main island and scale the towering cliffs; the winner being the first to present an unbroken egg to the tribal elders. Many fell to their death from the cliff faces, others drowned in the violent seas, and it certainly didn't help that these seas hosted sharks as well. These crazy scenes are depicted in cave paintings nearby.

There was just enough time to generate one more outstanding memory of Easter Island; not man-made this time, but remarkable natural beauty. Clare and I took a walk around the crater of Rano Kau. Almost a mile across and near-perfectly circular, the crater held a massive volume of rainwater on which numerous island beds of totora reeds floated. The steep walls of the crater, sheltering its interior from strong winds, had created a natural, unique greenhouse microclimate, allowing many rare and threatened botanical species to thrive. Quite the most impressive volcanic crater I had ever seen on my travels.

* * *

So Easter Island had provided a quite unique sensory experience of man-made and natural wonders, but there was another reason we were there: we had a race to run, and now it was only 36 hours away. After a splendid empanada lunch recommended by Hugo as the finest on the island, Clare and I decided to go for an exploratory run together around Hanga Roa, if only to wake our legs up a bit. Clare was still insistent that we should enjoy the experience of running the Rapa Nui half-marathon together. After our parkland run in Santiago, I found myself having to work quite hard trying to keep up with her and suggested we ran our own races, but she still maintained that we should do it together.

This time we set off in warm and muggy conditions down the hill towards the sea, turning right along the coastline, and looping around a colourful and decorative cemetery. We then started to tackle some of the hills in Hanga Roa and, once again, I was really struggling to keep pace with my running friend and by the time we finished our three-mile run, I was certain that I would be holding Clare back on the big day. This was her first major overseas running event, and I really wanted her to do the very best she could. I tentatively raised the subject again and this time was relieved to hear Clare agree that we should run our own races. It was only later, when I was preparing to shower after the run, that I discovered another reason why I might have struggled so much on those hills. In what was becoming the latest in a line of senior moments as I enter my later years, I had somehow run in my heavier trail walking shoes rather than my usual trainers. I have never done it before, nor have I since, but my mind must have been elsewhere when I kitted up.

Later that evening, with our little group of American friends, we sat on a grassy slope and watched a glorious, golden, red and purple sunset behind the five moai on Ahu Tahai on the shoreline of Hanga Roa. If ever a moment was made for photography, then that was it.

* * *

Pre-race day was largely given over to relaxation although the weather had taken a turn for the worse with increasingly stormy winds and heavy rain showers battering the wooden chalets at our hotel and spreading debris from the trees around the gardens. After a leisurely breakfast, Jacqui came round to distribute our individual race packs which she had collected on behalf of the whole group, as the planned pre-race packet pick-up activities had now become a paid event. It was becoming increasingly clear that there were tensions between the race organisers and the Marathon Tours party, but Jacqui was doing a sterling job on our behalf at the sometimes tetchy interface. Hugo, in particular, was bemused at the way we were being treated in comparison to other competitors.

There was also a mountain bike race around the island on that day which two Australian members of our party, Charlie and Tory, had entered, and after a very filling lunch, we gathered at the finish line to cheer them home. Hats off to them both, and particularly to Tory, who would be taking on the full marathon just a day later.

That evening our party found a local restaurant for our own pre-race pasta meal with not the friendliest of welcomes from the poor waitress who seemed to be working on her own, but who took out her frustrations on her paying customers with a rather feisty display. I guess that on such a small island, with so few visitors, she rarely had to deal with so many people all at once.

* * *

And so to race day, and almost uniquely in the running calendar, it began with a visit to church. After a light breakfast we walked up the hill from our hotel to the Holy Cross Catholic Church to attend a mass in the Rapa Nui language, a tradition of the Easter Island races. It was indeed a very uplifting experience with traditional costumes, singing and chanting, and powerful music with a strong percussive element. For me at least, it began to get the competitive juices flowing.

After slipping out of the service, which still had some time to run, we took a leisurely walk down to the coastline, pausing briefly at our hotel for that all-important last-minute toilet stop. The weather had been kind to us. The rain of the previous day had been displaced by sunshine and the fierce wind by a cooling breeze. On my left arm, I had a tattoo. Not a permanent one, although I'm quite sure there were people on the island capable of providing that service. Claire, the one with an 'i', had bought a selection of temporary tattoos from a local shop and had offered us each one. I had chosen the motif of the Birdman of Orongo, wistfully hoping that it might give me some positive encouragement and strength when the going got tough.

It was hectic down by the starting arch, overlooked by the single restored moai at Hanga Piko harbour. Street dogs, and there were plenty of them in Hanga Roa, mingled with the runners, photobombing many a souvenir start photo. The whole Marathon Tours contingent lined up for a group photo and then we were called to the start. All four distances were beginning at the same time on what was essentially an out-and-back route. I lined up well to the back, so as not to be overrun by the eager beavers, most of them local, running the shorter distances. On the given signal we were away, and another fabulous exotic running experience was about to be enjoyed, or perhaps endured, if it didn't go quite according to plan. Rather as I expected, Clare ran away from me immediately after the start, and I was pleased that we were both going to give it our best.

If I am to be brutally honest, and it's my story so I will be, the route was a little bit of an anti-climax. After an initial circuit of Hanga Roa town, which at least had some crowd support and included a very testing hill in the first mile, we followed the coastline around the harbour, and then went inland, past the airport, and then turned left to follow a very straight road that crossed the island in a north-easterly direction. The magic and beauty of Easter Island is largely focused around its coastal regions and it seemed a pity that at least part of the route could not have been on the coastal roads, with sightings of the magnificent moai to spur us along. But what do I know? Maybe the logistics of this would have made it impractical and, in any case, here I was running a race on a tiny dot in the middle of the Pacific Ocean that very few people would ever get to experience.

Barely had I reached the airport when the leaders of the 5km race were heading back towards me on the opposite side of the road. Once we made the turn inland the road ahead began to climb upwards, not particularly steeply, but absolutely relentlessly. The breeze was behind us, not really offering any cooling, and the heat began to be rather uncomfortable. I had chosen not to run with my Camelbak, which I frequently do in hot locations, so the first drink station just beyond the 5km mark was very welcome. I had decided to run instead with my flexible gel flask in my hand which had served me so well in the Antarctic. These were very different weather conditions but the gel flask offered a convenient and environmentally friendly way of mid-race fuelling.

Just beyond the aid station was the marshalled turning point for the 10km race, so a further surge of runners was passing back along the other side of the road, and the runners still heading uphill were now fewer. There was little to see; very pleasant rural countryside, only the occasional building or outhouse, and just once in a while a vehicle would trundle past us on the road: speed limits were strictly controlled on the island. There were cattle grazing in the meadows on either side of the road, but no fencing to restrict their movement; they just wandered freely. Just occasionally, a random chicken would appear, pecking for insects on the grassy verges.

Still the route climbed relentlessly towards its high point in the centre of the island. The full marathon runners, including Drew, would then continue on down to the coastline at Anakena before turning and having to climb back to the summit again on their return journey. I didn't envy them.

After another refreshing pause at the 10km drink station, I continued climbing in the knowledge that our turn-around point for the half-marathon would be soon after the seven-mile mark – we wouldn't be running the loop of Hanga Roa on the return leg, if you are questioning my maths. Shortly after the refreshment stop, I spotted Clare running towards me on the opposite side of the road. She was looking strong, told me that the turning point was not too far away, and we exchanged greetings and mutual encouragement.

Clare was right. In just a couple of minutes I was making a 180-degree turn, moving to the opposite side of the road, and what a difference it made. Now the gradient was downwards and the cooling breeze was in my face. It was time to push on a bit.

Before long it was my turn to shout encouragement to my running friends still battling uphill on the other side of the road. Among them, Megan, Charlie, Kate, Liz, Catharine and Kathy were climbing towards the turning point on their own half-marathon journey, and the amazing Claire with an 'i' and Drew were only about a quarter of the way through their full marathon. As I continued to enjoy the gradual descent, another familiar face came into view: our amazing tour guide, Jacqui, who was out on the course with her Marathon Tours flag, encouraging her runners to keep going until the very end.

And then there was a sort of confrontation with another of Easter Island's most famous attractions, arguably second only to the moai. The island was home to thousands of wild horses, and a large group of them was heading up the road that I was running down, directly towards me. I kept well to the side of the road but they barely gave me a second glance as they trotted by.

In the final couple of miles I began to struggle with quite severe calf cramps – maybe as a result of not taking on enough electrolyte during the rather unexpected heat in the first half of the race. No matter how many years you have been running for, you are never too old to learn lessons. As I had grown older, calf issues seemed to be becoming a feature of my longer runs, and it was at that moment that I made a mental note that calf compression sleeves would become part of my essential kit for all of my future long races.

As I turned the final bend, I could see the green finish arch a couple of hundred metres away from me. I did my best impression of a finishing sprint, crossing the line in a few seconds over two hours and 17 minutes and being immediately presented with my finishers' medal. To this day I am still amused by my finish-line photo which shows the race clock displaying a time of two hours, 17 minutes and 73 seconds! Perhaps Easter Island has its own unique time scale as well?

Clare was there at the finish for me with a drink and banana in hand, and four cups of orange squash and two bananas later I almost felt human again. We waited to see our other half-marathoners home and then it was back to the hotel for a much-needed shower, into a bar for a well-deserved beer and then back to the finish arch, to cheer home the amazing Claire and Drew as they finished their full marathon journeys.

* * *

The early evening, and rather lengthy, award presentations took place the same day in the local gymnasium, amid quite a lot of pomp and ceremony and another heavy percussive musical background. On checking the official results as we went in, I noted that both Clare and I had won our individual age categories, entitling us to a further gold medal award. On her own admission, Clare is not someone who relishes attention and she looked positively embarrassed as the gold medal was hung around her neck, as she stood on top of the podium with the runner-up and third-place finisher beside her. My award ceremony was a little more subdued. Although I was very pleased to have won my 70+ age category, I was the only person in that age group, being the oldest runner in the half-marathon race. I stood alone on the number one podium to receive my gold medal, but feeling internally satisfied that overall, I had finished in 29th position in the half-marathon in a field of 69. Yet another memorable running adventure was under my belt.

Chapter 4

Hotel déjà-vu

ONCE THE awards ceremony was over, Jacqui had arranged for the Marathon Tours party to have their own celebration meal in a nearby restaurant. It had been a very challenging trip, not least for Jacqui, but there were clearly major issues to sort out between our travel company and Rodrigo and his team of Chilean organisers. Quite what had been going on behind the scenes we would never know, nor was it really any of our business, but – to their credit and true to their word – Marathon Tours paid us a generous compensation package on our return home for the features that had been promised, but which they had been unable to deliver.

To be perfectly honest, the last-minute change of hotel and the loss of other social events linked to the race series did not spoil the trip one iota for me, and Easter Island will forever remain in my memory. Perhaps most tellingly of all, Marathon Tours announced that they would not be returning to the Easter Island race series in the future – a pity in so many ways as the island has so much to offer runners with an adventurous spirit.

At the meal, Jacqui gave a touching speech to thank us all for our patience and understanding and then presented each of us with a tiny ceramic turtle as a token of her gratitude. A great tour leader and one I would hope to run with again.

For many this was the end of the journey, as the following morning they would begin the long flight home. However, for me and a few others, including Clare and Drew, when you have travelled so far across the planet to live your adventure you may as well stay a bit longer and enjoy other scenic opportunities in that part of the world. We would be off to spend a few days in Peru, notably Machu Picchu, and the good news was that Jacqui would still be our tour leader.

* * *

As ever, our final few hours on Easter Island the following day did not go according to plan. News came through that the inbound flight from Santiago, which would be taking us back to Chile, had had to turn back because of a mechanical problem. We had a few more hours to play with than expected, and some of us took a walk out to the local brewery with the hope of perhaps a quick tour and maybe even a sample. We were accompanied all the way on the walk by a limping street dog but, alas, the brewery was closed for cleaning, so our hopes were dashed. We walked back, along with our loyal but lame new friend, who Jenny took pity on, and so she popped into a local shop to buy it some ham. This was dispatched in no time! We paused again at the church that we had visited on the morning of the race as Clare wanted to look around. Sadly, it too was closed for cleaning and, as I sat outside on the steps taking in my final few memories of Hanga Roa, our new faithful canine friend came and plonked himself across my lap and enjoyed a bit of a fuss.

There was still enough time for a final empanada and a couple of beers with Hugo, who also gave us each a little gift to remember him by – a small wooden moai to hang around our necks, a Rapa Nui symbol of safety on our future travels. Then it was time to move on.

When we finally landed back in Santiago, it was in the early hours of the morning and with a 4.30am alarm call booked for our next flight onwards to Lima it was, without doubt, the shortest time span between a hotel check-in and check-out I will ever have.

* * *

Machu Picchu was everything I had expected and more, much more. There can be few people who can't conjure up an image in their mind of this distinctive, 15th-century Incan citadel, perched upon a mountain ridge high up in the Peruvian Andes, but when you view it for the first time with your own eyes it sucks your breath away. The remoteness of its location, the intricacies of its construction, the overwhelming awesomeness of the steep, forested mountain peaks surrounding it, make it look both impenetrable but, at the same time, exposed.

Abandoned during the 16th-century Spanish conquest of Peru, although never actually discovered and plundered by the colonists, it remained hidden from the outside world until 1911, when the American historian Hiram Bingham came across the 'Lost City of the Incas' on his explorations, although he did not initially recognise the true extent of it as it was so overgrown with vegetation.

But before even getting to Machu Picchu, I had fallen a little bit in love with another Peruvian city that I had long wanted to visit, Cusco. Our flight from Santiago to Lima had been quickly followed by a much shorter flight inland to Cusco, high in the Andes mountains, and what was a spine-tingling descent to the airport with our pilot skilfully manoeuvring around imposing and, seemingly, extremely adjacent mountain peaks.

Cusco is located at an altitude of 3,400m – about 11,200ft – above sea level, and the watchword before even considering travelling there is 'altitude sickness', caused by the much lower levels of oxygen in the air that you breathe in. I had long ago decided that my running trainers would not be making an appearance while I was in Cusco. I have coped with running in extremely hot conditions as well as in the bitter cold but I still retain the memory of the struggles for breath that I experienced running at around 3,000m in the foothills of Tibet, back in 2000, and I was a lot younger and fitter then.

Readers of *Running Hot & Cold* may recall that back in 2008 I was within days of embarking on a series of adventure runs in the Andes, in Peru, Bolivia and

Chile, when I was forced to withdraw with previously undiagnosed high blood pressure. Thankfully, that has responded well to treatment which I will need to take for the rest of my life, but the possible consequences of running at altitude with such a condition were forcefully drummed home to me by my medical advisers. And as if I needed any more persuading, just a few years previously a very fit and young running friend, who had been part of our party to the race in Myanmar in 2014, visited Cusco on a trekking holiday and ended up in an intensive care bed in the local hospital, although he is now happily fully recovered.

From the moment we arrived in Cusco, our Peruvian tour guides were urging us to follow some basic guidelines to ward off altitude sickness, particularly during the first 24 hours when the body was adapting. We were advised to drink plenty of water, take everything slowly and avoid anything energetic. At the airport, trays of coca leaves were everywhere. Chewing coca leaves is a remedy the locals rely on heavily and all hotels had hot coca tea constantly available. Even our splendid hotel room had supplementary oxygen piped into it, and if the warnings weren't enough, walking slowly up a short flight of stairs soon reinforced why the precautions were so necessary.

But Cusco was a gem that epitomised all the pictures I had in my mind about Peru. It was colourful and completely chaotic in some parts, serene and peaceful in others. Road traffic was frenetic; on a guided tour of the city we were repeatedly transferred from vehicle to vehicle depending on both the width and the gradient of the streets we were about to explore. A moment of quiet reflection, observing the magnificent colonial Spanish architecture surrounding the vast expanses of the Plaza de Armas, was broken by the boisterous shouting and placard waving of a nurses' strike march. In a quieter square in the San Blas district, an interaction between two street dogs brought a smile to my face. An overly plump male was pursuing a much smaller female with obvious amorous intentions. The female squeezed through the open bars of a metal fence and then sat immediately behind it, facing her pursuer as if to say, 'Get through that, fatty!'

The beautiful grounds and gardens of Santa Domingo Church were another stunning highlight of the city. Built on what had been the Incan Temple of the Sun, Qorikancha, the throne of many Incan leaders, the wealth of gold and precious stones it had contained was unimaginable before the Spanish took Cusco in 1533.

And then there were the parades. We were approaching the time of the winter equinox festival and rehearsals were in full flow. Children during the daytime, adults in the evening and the costumes were as colourful and varied as could possibly be. Accompanied by marching bands, some of the children were barely old enough to walk, but coaxed along by adoring parents they seemed to revel in the attention of the watching crowds. And these were only the rehearsals! I would love to have been there on the big day itself.

As we moved out of the more affluent parts of the city in its central districts, and climbed even higher into the towering hillsides surrounding it, abject poverty became dominant as we drove past buildings that were no more than shanty towns. We reached the Inca ruins of Sacsayhuaman, at the opening of the descent into the Sacred Valley. Pronounced by many as 'sexy woman', this huge fortress overlooks the city of Cusco and is a marvel of ancient construction techniques with immense stones, each weighing dozens of tons, sculpted and joined together with absolute precision, so they fit tightly like giant medieval Lego. Indeed, it was the meticulousness of this rock work that had been one of the reasons why Thor Heyerdahl believed the Incas were the first settlers of Easter Island, as it so closely resembled the *ahu* we had seen for ourselves at Vinapu. As we wandered through the meadows surrounding the fortress, women and children in traditional Peruvian costume wandered by, with their family llamas in tow.

Our bus continued on down the Sacred Valley to Chinchero where we visited a llama and alpaca farm, as well as a demonstration by local ladies of how the wool was coloured by natural dyes and woven into the beautiful fabrics, sweaters and scarves for which Peru is so famous. On we travelled through the Urubamba Valley, stunning river scenery overlooked by snow-capped mountains, before arriving in Ollantaytambo where we boarded the train, the final leg of our journey to Machu Picchu, or at least to Aguas Calientes, the town at the foot of the mountain upon which the ancient city sits.

* * *

We had two days in which to explore Machu Picchu. All entry to the site is ticketed to limit visitor numbers at any one time and, with no bathroom facilities inside the citadel, the amount of time you can spend sightseeing is limited by the strength of your bladder. But first you have to get up there, and we joined the long bus queues in Aguas Calientes for the trip up the mountain road, the drivers skilfully negotiating their vehicles around a succession of spine-tingling hairpin bends.

Once we reached the car park outside of the site we again joined queues, this time for that all-important final toilet stop. Once our entrance tickets had been stamped, a re-admission on the same day was not permitted, we followed our Peruvian guide for a tour of the city. Any tour of such a mountainous location is bound to be strenuous but it is important to point out that, as lofty as it is, Machu Picchu is 1,000m lower than Cusco, so at least we had more oxygen to fuel our efforts.

I said it before, and I'll say it again, Machu Picchu was absolutely stunning. Whether it was the first sight of the ruins from up above, or walking through the remains of the ancient habitations and locations of religious and cultural significance, this just has to be one of the most fascinating places I have ever visited, and our tour guide truly enhanced the experience. A sturdy watch tower was perched on top of the massive Incan terraces that defended the city, and despite centuries of fearsome mountain weather, the ancient construction techniques have most certainly stood the test of time. Add to that the grandeur of the huge surrounding mountain peaks, and this is most certainly one of those places that no single photograph could ever do justice.

* * *

On our second day in the city, our tour guide offered us the choice of a challenging hike up Machu Picchu mountain to view the ruins from an even greater height, or a day exploring the surrounding panorama by ourselves. Although I had previously conquered my fear of heights by climbing Sigiriya rock in Sri Lanka, and indeed reaching the very summit of Sydney Harbour Bridge, I did have a degree of protection from both companions and equipment on both occasions. After hearing a description of the route I, along with several others including Jacqui, Clare and Drew, decided to opt for the self-exploration alternative. On hearing later that a couple of people who took on the mountain hike had been forced to turn back, I felt I had made the right choice, for me at least.

In my quest for running adventure over the preceding years, one race that had seriously tempted me was the Inca Trail Marathon, finishing in Machu Picchu and organised by Devy Reinstein, owner of Andes Adventures. Sadly, during my working days, this fell at a time of year when I just couldn't take time off due to my teaching commitments. I had, of course, found a South American alternative when I entered Devy's Andes Triangle adventure back in 2009 but, as I mentioned earlier, that didn't end well. When visualising what it must have been like to finish the Inca Trail Marathon, the image I repeatedly conjured up in my mind was reaching the Sun Gate, Intipunku, above Machu Picchu, and looking down on the ruins for the very first time, before the descent down to the finish line. OK, this time I had reached the sacred city by the less arduous means of bus and train, but this did give me the opportunity to reverse that vision, and climb up the trail to the Sun Gate, so that I could at least see the view for myself.

In the company of good friends we climbed the rocky and uneven trail up the mountainside, pausing only to draw breath while taking a myriad of photographs or engaging in interaction with inquisitive llamas. There was the occasional section that turned my knees to jelly but it was well worth the magnificent view of the fabled city below.

On returning back down to the city, we still had time to visit what has been described as the 'back-door' entrance to Machu Picchu; the Inca bridge. Although safe if you are careful, the 30-minute trek out to the bridge was very narrow in parts, with precipitous drops just feet away. Just to be sure, as you enter the trail that leads to the bridge, there is a warden's hut at which you are required to sign in and sign out, to make sure that all those who go out do come back again. While the bridge itself is no longer accessible, entry being prevented by a very sturdy gate after a tourist reportedly fell to their death, the end of the trail does offer very clear views of what is little more than a narrow man-made shelf, with a short section that could only be traversed by walking across wooden planks, all attached to the side of a towering, vertical rock face with hundreds of feet of nothing but fresh air below it. It was beyond me how anyone had the courage to walk along it, and I cannot begin to imagine how many lives must have been lost during its construction.

* * *

As our train trundled back through the Sacred Valley towards Cusco, we were first served with a snack and a pisco sour, a local Peruvian cocktail. The multi-talented train crew then became fashion models as they paraded through the carriages wearing a variety of Peruvian clothing made of alpaca wool, and secured a few purchases for their troubles. And then their final transformation: donning animal masks, tousled wigs and the most colourful costumes imaginable, they treated us to a live Andean dancing show which even continued on to the platform at our final destination. You certainly earn your money if you work for PeruRail on the Machu Picchu train.

It had been a humbling and fitting end to our visit to some of the most extraordinary locations I have ever visited. Combined with the wonders of Easter Island, it had been a fortnight of disbelief and head-shaking at just how, so many centuries ago, and without the construction and transport tools we have at our disposal today, these buildings and artefacts had been created and moved in the most inhospitable of environments.

* * *

I have already explained my decision why I chose not to run in the oxygen-sparse heights of the Andes, but it would have been rude not to put on my trainers at some point on a visit to Peru. Fortunately, Clare and I had half a day free in the coastal capital, Lima, as we began our long journey back home; time for a short but chaotic, traffic-dodging, pre-breakfast city run. Judging by the looks that we got from both locals and the police, running on the streets of Lima was not a common early morning pastime. After our run a few hours remained for a more sedate tour of the city's cathedral, and to the gates of the presidential palace. They are wonderful in their own right but, for me, Peru will always be about the magical charm of Cusco and Machu Picchu.

* * *

With one island completed of my 2019 challenge, attention now turned to what was looking a pretty relentless autumn schedule with trips to the Azores, Venice and Cyprus. Priority had to be maintaining my fitness, with the odd niggle and strain seemingly becoming more common as I grew older, but at the same time trying to up the mileage so as to be marathon-ready for the big one in Venice: a bit of a balancing act.

On the family front, things were beginning to look a bit better for Chris. Although he was still getting the shadow attacks, the excruciating cluster headaches seemed to have subsided since his nerve block procedure. He was, however, not out of the woods yet and eager to learn as much as possible about the condition, which he knew was likely to return at some point in the future. He asked me if I would join him at a one-day conference arranged by the Organisation for the Understanding of Cluster Headache (aptly abbreviated to OUCH) on a Sunday, late in June, at St Thomas' Hospital in London. Targeted at sufferers, their families and health professionals alike, Chris thought my presence might help with the more scientific and medical aspects of the presentations. This, of course, I was happy to do but it did make for one of the more onerous weekends of my life.

The day before the meeting in London, I had accepted an invitation to attend the Riverside parkrun in County Durham, before giving a presentation of my running travels and books as part of the Derwent Valley Literature Festival. It meant a drive of more than 200 miles on the Friday afternoon, a similar distance back to Telford after the run and talk were finished to meet up with Chris, before a disrupted train journey down to London, to arrive just in time for a pint before the pubs closed. It was hectic but it was worth it, both from the literary and medical points of view.

There was also further summer movement on the booking of future events; you already know how easily convinced I am when opportunities to race abroad are offered, particularly after a glass of wine! The bonds formed with some of our American friends from the Easter Island adventure were such that we were all eager to meet up again as soon as possible at another event. With our friends from across the pond eager to come to Europe, the Prague half-marathon in March 2020 seemed to fit with most people's diaries, so this was booked.

And then I was tempted once again, this time with the Bermuda Triangle Challenge in January 2020. Three races on successive days: a one-mile dash, certainly not a natural distance for me, a 10km race, and then a half-marathon. The appeal for me was that it was another island. OK, it fell a couple of weeks beyond 2019 but who was counting? With a click of a mouse, my 'four islands, ten races, 100 miles' challenge had extended to 'five islands, 13 races, 120 miles'. Catharine, Liz and Drew were happy to sign up too and once again, with Bill's blessing, as this flight would have been too long for him, Clare was happy to share the trip with me.

* * *

While I knew that the two four-day challenges in the Azores and Cyprus would be particularly tough, with such short recovery times in between each stage, it was the prospect of running the full marathon distance again after a break of seven years that triggered the most stomach butterflies. It was not an easy preparation period for my running buddy Julie either. So often there for me in the past when I had been struggling with mental wellbeing issues, she was now fighting her own mind battles as she coped with significant turmoil in her family and work life. We made an unlikely but mutually supportive partnership, given the considerable age difference between us but, as a run leading team, we were strong and vowed to urge each other through.

As I trained through the summer months, there was something a little disconcerting that seemed to be creeping into my running diary entries, rather more frequently than I would have liked, and that was taking a mid-run tumble. I have always maintained that you are not a real runner unless you have taken a tumble or two. Over the course of my running life, there were usually one or two occasions a year when a toe caught a kerb or perhaps a tree root and you suddenly found yourself 'kissing the tarmac'. I have always had a fairly low foot lift, and while this can be economical in terms of energy expenditure, it does leave you a bit susceptible to uneven surfaces. In the vast majority of cases, it has just led to cuts and grazes on my hands, knees and elbows, and only on a couple of occasions has my head or face made contact with the ground, which can cause some temporary disruption to one's facial features!

Having already taken a few tumbles earlier in the year, I managed to fall twice on a seven-mile training run with Julie. No lasting damage was done but I knew it was a bit disconcerting for Julie, who felt a bit responsible for this old guy she was running with who couldn't stay upright. It did knock my confidence, and it meant I had to focus much more on keeping my feet up. Hopefully it was just a passing phase rather than an inevitable consequence of ageing.

* * *

Almost before I knew it, I was hauling myself out of bed at some unearthly hour in the middle of the night, ready to drive down to Stansted for the flight out to the Azores. With such a busy schedule of events ahead, the pennies had to be spent wisely and I'd opted for the very early start from home to save the expense of an airport hotel stay. This was going to be one of those events where I was travelling alone, and probably knew none of the touring party, other than Mike Gratton, who was leading the group. I had also opted for the cheaper option of room-sharing with an unknown competitor, something I had done on many past adventures, and always with a good outcome. Somehow runners always seem to be easy to get on with, even when you've never met before.

The flight was pretty uneventful, apart from my spotting the ID card of a Spanish lady under the seat in front of me. I passed it to the cabin crew who made an announcement, but the lady in question was not on board. It must have been from a previous flight; someone was having a difficult morning somewhere!

I looked around to see if I could spot anyone else who looked as if they might be flying out for the race series rather than for just a holiday break, but how can you tell? We runners come in all shapes, sizes and age groups. I did spot a lady who was reading a running magazine and, as it happened, that would have been a correct guess. On arrival at the João Paulo II Airport, on the island of São Miguel, I hired a friendly taxi driver who took me to the door of the harbourside hotel, in the main town of Ponta Delgada, which would be our race headquarters as well as hosting the post-race celebration meal.

Almost simultaneously another eight people arrived and, for the first time, we were able to introduce ourselves to each other as fellow runners. One by one we gave our names to the hotel receptionist who tapped away at her keyboard with a quizzical look on her face.

'I'm sorry, I can't find your booking,' she said each time, and then she called the hotel manager. He repeated the keyboard typing, and waded through reams of white paper in a folder. More head-shaking. We contacted the office of 2:09 Events back in the UK and were assured that the hotel booking had been confirmed. This was the same hotel that had hosted the small pilot event the previous year, and all would be sorted imminently when Mike Gratton himself arrived with the paperwork. Mike, and a few others, had flown from Gatwick via Lisbon, and had landed only an hour behind us.

Soon Mike was at the desk, and he produced the hotel confirmation. The penny dropped. The agents in Ponta Delgada who handled the hotel booking for 2:09 Events had mistakenly booked a different hotel with a very similar name, and nobody had noticed. For the second time in just a few months, we were not to be in the hotel we had paid for!

As I said after the hotel fiasco of Easter Island, this was really not a problem for me. Just as long as we had an alternative, and I had a bed to rest my head, then all would be fine. Mike hastily arranged for a small fleet

93

of taxis to take us all to our new base. It was perfectly adequate, and I even discovered I'd been given a room to myself, at no extra cost, as there was no one suitable to share with. The hotel was not as salubrious as our intended destination but was instead what I would describe as a conference hotel with rather more basic facilities. Where it did fall short, however, was in its location. Whereas our planned hotel was right on the waterfront, and close to all the bars and restaurants, this one was a kilometre inland. To long-distance runners you might think that a kilometre is nothing, but this was a very steep uphill kilometre from the coast, and it was waiting to challenge us each time we returned from an evening out!

Not the best start, but not the end of the world either and, just a short time after my return home from this trip, I once again received another generous compensation payment. It all helped to fund future events.

Chapter 5

Running on a seafood diet

ANYONE READING this who knows me personally will recognise that I am quite a reserved person who seldom makes the first move when it comes to meeting new people I have not met before; a little bit socially awkward, you might say. At the end of another day full of surprises, and without a room buddy to get to know, I took myself off down to the harbour for a brief exploratory tour, before taking on that hill for the very first time on the climb back up to the hotel.

The following day was pretty much at leisure with just the race briefing in the evening. Despite having a four-day running event looming, it just seemed the right thing to do to blow away any remaining travel cobwebs, and reconnoitre Ponta Delgada in my running shoes. After relishing the first downhill kilometre to the harbour in warm but overcast conditions, I headed east along the largely flat coastal road, the footpath being separated from a parallel cycle path by beautifully manicured and colourful flower beds. It all seemed so clean and well-maintained. The shoreline itself was protected against the constant battering of the Atlantic waves by a combination of natural boulders and huge man-made concrete, tripod-shaped structures that knitted together. Balanced precariously on top, local fishermen cast their lines into the raging waters below.

After a mile or so I reached an impressive viewpoint looking out over to the islet of Rosto de Cão, a striking rock formation jutting out into the sea and split asunder by historic volcanic activity. I retraced my footsteps back towards the central area and onwards around the inner harbour arm, containing a sheltered and supervised swimming area and lined with enticing restaurants. I was impressed. The Azores was never really a part of the world I had considered for family holidays, but first impressions were positive. My enthusiasm may have dimmed slightly as I laboured back up that damned hill to the hotel, even having to take a pause for a breather on a particularly steep session, but I was sufficiently galvanised to repeat the route that same afternoon, this time at walking pace and armed with a camera to capture some of the memories.

The evening race briefing was a bit of an eye-opener in that it was the first time I realised just how small an event this was going to be in terms of participant numbers. Just 56 competitors in total, many of them native Azoreans, and there were only 15 of us from the UK. I was allocated number 37. As I had seen in Cyprus back in 2016, Mike Gratton's briefing was just about as informative as you can get, with detailed descriptions of each of the four races including route maps and elevation profiles. First impressions? Races one and three looked relatively straightforward, but two and four looked a whole lot more challenging. Time would tell.

* * *

A little digression here. From the moment I became an author, with the publication of *Running Hot & Cold*, I also became a public speaker, some may say inspirational, recounting my many adventures on my running travels around the world. These talks cover all age ranges: primary and secondary school children, colleges and universities, athletics clubs and a variety of adult groups including Rotary clubs, Women's Institutes and many others. If you have read my previous books, you may even recall a talk inside a prison. At the end of each session I like to give the audience the chance to ask questions. With children, these are usually about the animals I have come across on my journeys, but with adults, and particularly the more senior age groups, by far the most common question is 'How are your knees?' Thankfully, and touching wood, they have held up pretty well so far, apart from a couple of minor strains.

Another question I am frequently asked, by all age groups, is whether I need a special diet to sustain all the running. I like to be light-hearted with my presentations, so my usual response is, 'I follow a seafood diet – if I see food, I eat it!' The old jokes are the best! I am lucky in that I enjoy eating just about anything and, happily, don't have a corresponding weight problem, but the reason I raise this here is that the Azores, out there in the North Atlantic, has a large fishing industry and its restaurants are renowned for their seafood dishes.

After the race briefing had finished, I made my way back down that hill to the restaurants on the harbour arm and finally made my choice from a wide selection. I was not disappointed; how often do you finish a restaurant meal, sit back, and just think, 'Wow'? The sea bass was cooked to perfection, as were the sweet potato mash and mixed vegetables. I justified the dessert of a chocolate brownie, chocolate ice-cream and fresh cream on the basis I was on holiday and washed the whole lot down with a cool pint of local beer – a 'see food' diet at its finest.

* * *

And so to race number one and, as with the Cyprus 4-Day Challenge, this was a relatively gentle introduction to the series; a mostly flat 5km run along coastal paths, most of which I had run the previous day. If it had been a Saturday morning it would have made a perfect parkrun route, but it was a Monday.

We walked down to the start on the lower promenade in warm early morning sunshine. By now I had begun to get to know several of my fellow competitors and was joined by Helen, an NHS worker from Norfolk. Helen had travelled with her partner Stephen, who was a runner himself but currently out of action through injury. Mike Gratton, our race director, was joined by his brother Dave, and between them and their local liaison contact, a few very busy days lay ahead of them. Not only did they have to set out the route markers and signage for the current day's race, administer the start with all the usual safety briefings, time the finishers, process the results and then remove the signage, they then had to travel to another part of the island and set up the course and direction arrows for the following day's race, which on this occasion was a trail half-marathon. As if that wasn't enough, Dave was also acting as race photographer! Happily, they were able to get some assistance from some of the non-running partners of the competitors, including Stephen; many had travelled with Mike before and seemed to know him well.

As we mingled at the start, it was clear that there were some very serious runners taking part as they went through vigorous warm-up routines. Most of these seemed to be local athletes. At the other extreme there were a handful who planned to walk the whole series, so I was reassured I wouldn't be finishing last. Nevertheless, I placed myself towards the rear of the group as Mike counted us down to the start signal.

As expected, the leaders flew away from me at pace as we first headed west along the promenade, before climbing a ramp on to the walkways of the upper coast road and heading due east through the town. Although there were a few pedestrians around, it was still relatively early in the morning and, with such a small field, it was easy to negotiate a clear run through. My personal aim was to run a respectable parkrun time for me, but not to push myself too hard with three far more difficult stages ahead. I had had a bit of a pre-race warm-up, but as was becoming the way of things as I grew older and my joints became creakier, the early phases of the run would be a gradual loosening-up process and, for this distance at least, my kilometre splits would get progressively faster.

After a short climb towards the town centre, the route then levelled out as we headed on to the paved footpaths I had run along the previous day, although this time I was moving a whole lot faster. With colourful flowers to my left and the Atlantic waves crashing into the sea defences to my right, I was again relishing the inner tranquillity that running has brought to my life. Before too long the race leaders were storming back towards me on the other side of the flower beds at an amazing pace but I was content that I was doing myself justice. When I reached the turning point, we took a loop around Forno da Cal, a fortified 19th-century lime kiln that had been transformed into a viewing point overlooking the picturesque Rosto de Cão rock formation that I had admired and photographed the previous day.

I was heading back towards the finish and felt a slight sense of relief that there were still several other runners behind me. I was still gradually increasing my modest pace as the finish line came into sight when I spotted Dave with his camera, and put in a finishing burst that had me thankful for the bottle of cold water I was handed at the end. I had completed one quarter of the stages, but I was under no illusion that I had expended one quarter of the effort required to finish the whole series!

* * *

Our early start meant that even after the climb back up the hill to the hotel, and a much-needed shower, there was still time for a full English breakfast to top up energy supplies. I then went back down to the harbour and being the lover of nature in the wild that I am, booked myself an afternoon whale- and dolphin-watching trip. I knew with certainty that nothing was going to come anywhere near the experience I had had with the two humpback whales in the icy waters of Antarctica, but I nevertheless looked forward to the challenges of capturing some wildlife photography.

At the appointed time, I turned up at the boat terminal and was delighted to see that Helen's partner Stephen had booked on to the same trip; it would be good to have company. Helen herself had chosen not to risk seasickness the day before a half-marathon and decided to stay on dry land. The wind had increased quite a lot during the day and the seas were definitely a lot choppier; in fact, several of the local boat companies had cancelled their afternoon trips. Notwithstanding, I trusted that the sea legs that I had apparently grown on the return trip from Antarctica across the Southern Ocean would still be there and be capable of being tossed around for a couple of hours in a fairly rough Atlantic.

After a safety briefing video inside the cabin of our vessel, Stephen and I moved up on to the deck as we left the shelter of the harbour walls and out into open water, cameras at the ready. I had decided to take my single-lens reflex camera, fitted with a telephoto lens, and set to continuous shooting. It was a strategy that worked. Let me say first that we did not encounter a single whale on the trip but, as I said before, this was not a huge disappointment to me. We did, however, encounter several pods of both striped and Atlantic spotted dolphins. Interestingly, at least for me, these would actually be identified by on-shore spotters with powerful binoculars, who would then relay the location to the boat's captain. Local regulations allowed the captain to reach the pod and then shut off the engine for a few minutes to allow us to get some photographs, before starting up again and leaving these wonderful creatures in peace.

Taking the photos was no easy feat as the boat was tossed from side to side by the turbulent waves. It was a matter of coordinating hanging on to something solid for dear life, bracing your legs to avoid becoming a human projectile across the deck, pointing the camera in a direction you hoped the dolphins would take, and keeping an index finger on the shutter button. Of hundreds of resulting photos, just a handful managed to avoid being sent immediately to the recycle bin, but the few that survived made the whole experience worthwhile. Nature at its finest – watching the apparent joy of these dolphins as they leapt in and out of the waves on the open sea, and no comparison at all to the sight of captive dolphins, confined to a small pool and being encouraged to perform tricks to entertain their human onlookers.

Once back on dry land, Stephen and I stopped by a local bar for a couple of cool beers and were joined by Geoff, another one of the British running contingent, and one of very few who were in the privileged position of knowing what was to come, as he had taken part in the pilot event the year previously. Geoff was happy to reaffirm that 'you ain't seen nothing yet'.

Another sumptuous meal and then it was an early night for me. The following morning the Sete Cidades volcano half-marathon was lying in wait.

* * *

After a light breakfast, we gathered in the hotel foyer to wait for the coaches that would take us to the volcanic complex of Sete Cidades at the western end of São Miguel Island. In a year when nothing much was going to plan, it really wasn't very surprising when they didn't show up at the designated time of 8am. Forty minutes later a coach did pull up outside and we rushed out to board, only to discover that it was booked for another party staying at the hotel. By now Mike and his Azorean counterparts were frantically on the phone trying to find out what was going on; maybe the people who had booked the wrong hotel had also arranged our transport.

Eventually, an hour after they were due, the coaches did arrive and we were finally on our way. What were we expecting to see? I am no volcanologist but had done a little bit of reading prior to my visit, partly out of curiosity and maybe a little bit down to personal safety issues. The complex was defined as a caldera, a circular hollow formed when the top of a volcano is blown off in an eruption, and the walls collapse in on themselves. Apparently three major eruptions occurred between 20,000 and 40,000 years ago, but several smaller eruptions have occurred since, the most recent being in the 15th century AD, which in geological terms was like 'last week', so the volcano was classed as dormant rather than extinct.

There were two features of the volcanic complex that made it an extraordinary and unique place to visit. The first was that at the base of this huge circular crater lay the small but thriving town of Sete Cidades! I just wonder who first thought that it might be a good idea to build a town in a dormant volcano, and I can only speculate on what insurance premiums must be like. The second unique feature was the huge lagoon that filled the entire crater but that was divided into two by a narrow road bridge. On one side of the bridge the water is clearly blue in colour (Lagoa Azul), and on the other side it is green (Lagoa Verde) and I had seen many pictures of this prior to my visit. Several explanations had been put forward for this strange spectacle – the simplest being that this was just the physics of reflected light from the surroundings. Certainly, in the photographs I had seen that had been taken in bright sunlight, the contrast was vivid, but even in the overcast conditions on the day of our race the difference in colour either side of the bridge was still very noticeable. Other plausible reasons were differences in the chemical nature of the deposits beneath the lagoons, or even different micro-organisms living in the water on either side of the divide. Maybe a mixture of all three but, in any case, a very striking phenomenon.

Our coaches dropped us off in a remote hilly location, out of sight of the volcano itself. We were going to be starting rather later than planned but this was not really an issue. We were a relatively small group in an inaccessible locality and it wasn't as if Mike and his group of helpers had road closures to factor into their plans. No sooner had I stepped out of the coach than I noticed a ludicrously steep track heading up to a nearby peak, and remarked to Helen that this was going to be our route. I was joking, but I was spot on! We were led down a slope on to a narrow, dusty trail and lined up alongside the start banner that had been laid out the day before. Three, two, one, go.

From the very first step forward we were climbing, and it wasn't an easy gradient either. The very last thing I wanted to do on a tough, rough trail race was to give in to walking too soon, so I gritted my teeth and ploughed on upwards. The banks were high at the side of the trail so there wasn't much scenery to take my mind off the struggle, but after the longest half mile ever the gradient relented a little. It was a false dawn. Soon we were climbing again and now it was even steeper. My breathing sounded like a clapped-out steam locomotive and, with great reluctance, the urge to walk won the battle in my mind. Hands clamped to the front of my thighs, I forced myself up to the summit ahead and paused there for a second to give thanks for the next section which seemed to be slightly downhill. What a start and we were only one mile into the race.

I was still some way from the rim of the crater, but with so few runners in the race, and with such a wide range of running abilities, with me being at the slower end of the spectrum I was already pretty much alone and would remain so for the remainder of the race. After another mile or so the blue lagoon came into sight, although the far side of the crater was shrouded in mist. Underfoot it was a loose rocky trail, so I had to run with caution in mind with my increasing propensity to take a tumble. Happily the forecast thunderstorms had not materialised and I was grateful for that; I really wouldn't have enjoyed running on the rim of a volcano if there was lightning about. It was extremely windy though, and every now and again I would find myself enveloped in a swirling dust storm.

The scenery, and indeed the greenery, as I ran at the very rim of the crater was quite stunning: another beautiful example of what our planet has to offer. On a couple of occasions I met enthusiastic hikers coming the other way, and I was buoyed by their encouragement. Rather less helpful, but still very amusing, was coming face-to-face with a large herd of cattle being driven slowly down the trail by a local farmer in his four-wheel-drive vehicle. I took refuge in some bushes at the side of the track as they passed and received a toothless grin and a thumbs-up from the farmer in response.

At around the 10km mark I reached a short section of tarmac road and, shortly afterwards, one of the three drink stations provided by the local organisers. By now, I was regretting my decision not to have worn my Camelbak hydration pack for water en route, but to instead rely solely on my soft gel flasks for nutrition. The gels were working fine but the dry, dusty and windy conditions were leaving me really thirsty. I gulped down some much needed water, thanked the volunteers, and then headed up the signposted trail, and when I say up, I mean up! The next five kilometres was some of the toughest trail running I have ever done in my life; it was relentlessly in an upward direction. Underfoot, it was becoming more and more difficult to pick your way through the loose, rocky rubble, and the inevitable happened: I tripped and fell. Fortunately, running uphill meant that forward momentum was not very great, so little damage was done other than a few scratches and grazes, but it did knock my confidence.

Finally the trail levelled out and the summit came into view. Looking down to the left, I could now see the green lagoon and the village of Sete Cidades. The descent began and, at times, it was a very steep and treacherous one, involving navigating some sections on my backside; it was more of a plummet than a descent! The trail became firmer and smoother, the gradient gradually lessened and eventually became tarmac again and, before long, I was running with my normal posture again through the quaint town, the house gardens brimming with bright flowers. I ran across the road bridge that separated the two lagoons, and there was Dave with his camera, this time capturing me with a smile on my face now that I was back down to the level of the water.

With two kilometres to go I passed the coaches that would be taking us back to the hotel. Already faster runners were boarding, having finished the race and then walked that distance back to where the coaches were parked. Tarmac turned back to trail, although this was a relatively hard-packed and smooth surface as we ran out on to a promontory that jutted out into the blue lagoon. Geese and ducks bickered noisily at the water's edge, and wild, colourful hydrangea bushes were in abundance. I met Helen and Stephen walking back towards me, heading for the coaches, and despite the ever-increasing cramping in my calf muscles, that gave me a final boost to the point at which the finish banner came into view in the distance and I upped my pace for that final sprint, finishing with arms aloft and having my finish line photo taken by a former winner of the London Marathon, Mike.

There was still the 2km walk back to the last coach to negotiate; the earlier one had long since departed. Chastising myself for forgetting to put anti-chafing gel on those parts you know will suffer, I grabbed a drink, fruit and some snacks and ambled back slowly towards the pick-up point, stopping to take a few photos of some of the delightful scenes that had helped me get through those final stages. The experience had been magical, but it had really tested me to my limits, and I still had two stages to run.

* * *

It's fair to say that, when I woke early the following morning, I was suffering from the worst DOMS I could remember, probably since my runs in the Sahara over 20 years previously. For non-runners reading this, DOMS is an acronym for delayed onset muscle soreness, something that appears 12 to 24 hours after a really vigorous workout and is attributed to an inflammatory response of the body to the microscopic tears in muscle fibres resulting from the exercise. Whatever the cause, it really hurts and it was a hobbling version of me that crept down for an early breakfast. I was somewhat reassured to see that almost all of the other runners were having similar mobility issues as they filled their breakfast plates and, indeed, Helen agreed with me that the previous day's half-marathon was one of the very toughest races she had ever done.

Mercifully, the third race in the series was relatively short at 6.5km and also mostly flat. In contrast to the previous day, the coaches arrived bang on time and took us out to the town of Furnas in the eastern half of the island. Furnas is a small spa town famous for its geothermal activity and, no sooner had we stepped off the coach alongside a stunningly beautiful lake, the Lagao das Furnas, we could smell the sulphurous fumes in the air as steam rose from the many vents around us. As we traipsed through some woods towards the water's edge, stepping carefully over convoluted tree root systems, feral cats could be seen basking on the centrally heated soil; they looked as if they were in paradise.

Steep, green mountainsides towered above us and, all around, steam was rising from the many fumaroles of the hot springs. In one section the individual vents carried the names of local restaurants, and chefs would come and lower pots of their traditional dishes into the hot steam to cook them for their customers later in the day.

We gathered by a large, carved wooden statue of a mermaid at the edge of the lake. This particular race was to be run in a handicap format, with the slowest over the previous two days starting first. This meant that I didn't have too long to wait. One by one, or occasionally in pairs, Mike would call us to the start line and count us down to the signal to run. I lined up with Brendan, a retired RAF officer, and he shot ahead of me as we were sent on our way. The moment was captured perfectly by Dave with his camera to produce one of those photographs you will always treasure: Brendan racing away and yours truly, about two metres behind, framed perfectly by a giant plume of steam in the background, making it look as if I was having to work extremely hard to keep up which, in truth, I was. Those first few hundred metres were excruciating; my DOMS-ridden legs begging me to stop but my mind urging me to keep going in the sure knowledge that the pain would soon subside.

The first two kilometres was something of a roller-coaster ride on some rough dirt trail; an initial descent to a stream that had to be leapt over, followed by a series of ups and downs before the trail eventually levelled out and I could get a bit of rhythm into my running. The route would take us around the whole perimeter of the lake, finishing where we started, and there was so much wonderful scenery to admire that the discomfort in my legs became much less of an issue. Very occasionally I would pass one of the competitors who had started in front of me. Rather more frequently, a speedier runner would come by me on the sometimes narrow trail. At around four kilometres in we joined a track that ran alongside the road bordering the eastern side of the lake and this gave magnificent views of the hills and peaks to the west, with stunning reflections in the still waters. With less than a kilometre left to run we diverted away again from the road back on to hard-packed trail, and I was able to coax the speediest pace of the race out of my legs as Mike timed me across the finish line. Another race in the bag and just one more to go.

Before returning to our hotel we did spend a rather splendid few hours in the picturesque town of Furnas, with many taking advantage of a swim in the thermal pools of Terra Nostra Park. Being a non-swimmer myself, I satisfied myself by sitting on the edge for an hour and immersing my aching legs in the warm, brown water. The park itself was a delight, brimming with colourful flowers and plants, bubbling streams and lily-laden ponds, an abundance of fish and birdlife that I couldn't begin to identify, and the blue and white porcelain murals that were so typical of the island. In the town the tiny shops competed among themselves to be the most visually appealing, the fresh produce being displayed in multi-coloured wicker baskets outside vibrant shopfronts.

* * *

And so to the final race and, as anyone who has experienced severe DOMS will testify, the pain and discomfort can reach its peak around 48 hours after the causal event. The temporary relief I had felt as I progressed around the lake at Furnas the previous day was exactly that – temporary. Even as I walked around the park, movement was becoming more and more uncomfortable and I can vividly recall the struggle I had descending one flight of steps from the entrance to the town's church. As on the previous day, breakfast highlighted that I was far from the only competitor in this position, but a far sterner test lay ahead of us on this final day.

The Serra Tronquiera race was a 17km trail run starting on the slopes of São Miguel's highest mountain, Pico da Vara, and finishing in the town of Nordeste on the eastern coast of the island. Having learned from the mistake I had made on the volcano rim run, this time I did wear my hydration pack on my back, and it served me well in the very warm weather. The first 12 kilometres of this run would be held entirely on forest trail, which was hard-packed and reasonably smooth, although you always had to be on the lookout for the occasional protruding tree root or embedded rock just waiting to bring you down.

Mike set us on our way, this time en masse, and immediately the route started to climb, not as steeply as the initial section of the volcano run, but much more relentlessly. In fact, as we climbed towards the summit of Pico da Vara, the first five kilometres was entirely uphill and this was not what my legs needed. As on previous runs, for most of the time I was running alone, and this time the surroundings were really unique. I was running through what was known as a laurel forest, characteristic of subtropical regions with high humidity and fairly stable, mild temperatures the year round. At the side of the trail, evergreen and hardwood trees towered up towards the sky, producing a leaf canopy that kept the worst of the sun's rays off. For much of the time you could see nothing but endless, tightly packed tree trunks but every now and again, a gap would appear, and you could see far down to the lowlands below.

For the first two kilometres I managed to keep my aching legs running up the never-ending climb, although at a pretty pedestrian pace, but I then had to resort to a walk-run strategy where I would walk for 100 paces before then starting to run again for as long as I could. It got me through and, at the five-kilometre mark, I had reached the highest point of the race where we would no longer head up to the mountain summit, but would turn east and begin a slow and gradual descent towards the coast. Now I was moving slightly downhill, the surroundings seemed to become even more appealing and mentally uplifting. The trail twisted and turned in a series of zig-zags as I enjoyed the descent and every time the tree trunks parted a little to give me a brief view of the land below, it gradually crept that little bit closer.

Up ahead, I spotted a small group of forestry workers in their luminous safety jackets. They stood to either side to let me through, yelling encouragement as I passed, and delivered a rapid succession of high-fives, left and right. It is amazing what a lift these moments give you. At 12 kilometres I eventually emerged from the forest. Ahead, I could see the coastline but there was still a lot of descending to do as the now, much wider, trail continued to twist and turn. Only the distance of a parkrun to go and now I knew I would be completing the race series.

Did that thought cause me to relax a bit and lose concentration? Just before the 14-kilometre marker, I was suddenly face down in the dirt. Yes, yet another fall. If it had been a training run I would have immediately paused my Garmin watch and given myself a few minutes to recover, but this was a race and the clock was ticking. Unlike the fall on the volcano rim, when I had been running uphill, this tumble happened at a faster pace which consequently meant that blood had been spilled. I sat myself upright and quickly assessed which bits were hurting. I had avoided actually banging my head on the ground which was a good thing and there was no sign of any fracture; it just seemed to be superficial cuts and grazes, particularly on my left knee, but I was happy that I would be able to continue on to the finish.

As I prepared to start running again, a middle-aged Portuguese couple who were hiking up the trail approached me. They recoiled at the sight of the blood dripping off my leg and arm and, despite the language barrier, I was very firmly told to sit down again. As if by magic, the lady produced an emergency first aid kit from her rucksack and would simply not allow me to continue until she had cleaned all the dirt from the wounds with sterile wipes. I thanked them for their kindness and eventually set off again on the track that soon turned to tarmac as I entered the outskirts of Nordeste.

It was a long, straight downhill run to the finish line and I could see the cluster of runners standing there some time before I reached it. As I crossed the line, Mike placed the 4-Day Challenge medal over my head, wincing at the same time at the blood that was again flowing freely down my leg. Happily we had finished at a sports facility that had changing rooms and showers available, so I was soon able to get cleaned up again and to get some dressings on the damaged areas. The job was done; another four races of my islands challenge completed.

* * *

We stayed in Nordeste for a very pleasant buffet lunch, with wine of course now that the running was over, and I was introduced to one of the Spanish runners who was also a veteran of the Marathon des Sables, having run it three years previously. Again there was a language barrier but, nevertheless, a deep-seated mutual respect. That evening I walked down our infamous hill, with Helen and Stephen, to the hotel that we were originally intended to stay at, but that was still able to host our prize-giving dinner. With far fewer runners involved it was a relatively low-key affair compared to the Cyprus 4-Day Challenge but, nevertheless, the overall winner received very warm applause as he collected his trophy, and there was perhaps an even greater ovation when an 88-year-old Swiss lady was presented with a bottle of wine for her feat of having completed all four very tough stages. Of the 56 who started, 49 completed the full series and I was pleasantly surprised to have finished as high as 34th overall.

On reflection, the Azores experience exceeded my expectations in so many ways. The individual races were all so different from one another and the scenery was nothing short of spectacular. The volcano run will long live in my memory as one of the toughest half-marathons I have ever tackled. Of course, São Miguel was only one of the islands in the Azores, but there was no time for us to visit any of the others. As I said before, the Azores was never a place that was flagged up as a holiday destination in my family days but, having been there, I do wonder why.

And if you do decide to go, I would recommend the blue mouth fish too.

Chapter 6

Twenty-six point two

ANXIETY IS an insidious beast. There were fewer than five weeks between my returning from the Azores and then leaving our shores again for our group trip to the Venice Marathon. During that short period, I once again allowed my nerves to get the better of me. You know it is happening, you know your thoughts are misplaced, but it is so hard to just brush it all away.

I didn't make life easy for myself from the outset. The flight back from the Azores was severely delayed, so by the time I had arrived back at Stansted and then driven home it was close to midnight and I was pretty exhausted. As I pulled into the drive, my cat Nougat was in the front window and, recognising the car, became very animated. I quickly switched the engine off and went indoors to give her a hug as she always missed me when I was away. Mistake one: I left the car in gear! The following morning, and still feeling full of lethargy, I decided a drive to and a run around my local lake would shake some life back into me. Mistake two: I didn't check the gearstick was in neutral before I pushed the start button! The end result was that my shiny new car that I had only owned for a few weeks was now dented and damaged in a way that was, at least, fixable. Less lucky was the garage door, and that would have to be replaced. Not the homecoming I had planned and no one to blame but myself.

So why did the anxiety build? Apart from the extra hassle of getting the car and garage fixed, and sorting insurance claims, the very fact that a full marathon was looming on the horizon was certainly playing on my mind. You might think that after all the races I have taken part in, all around the planet, this would be something I would take in my stride. Not so; I even get butterflies in my tummy before a parkrun. My previous full marathon, in Rome, was now over six years ago. Perhaps I was marginally better prepared than I was for Rome, as I had taken that on at very short notice, but marginal was the key word here. I had no recent runs longer than half-marathon distance under my belt and, with time ticking away, I couldn't leave a longer run too long to give myself enough recovery time before the big day itself. I set myself a goal of a 16-mile run three weeks before departure. I chose a two-mile lapped route from my parked car, running it eight times in total, but giving me the opportunity to refuel and drink on a regular basis without having to carry supplies with me. And yes, I fell over once, although it was a part-grassy landing so little damage was done. I felt pretty pleased to have finished the session in a reasonable time but knew that it was not the preparation I would have liked. Pretty much as I had done in Rome, I would have to 'wing it' for the last ten miles.

As I alluded to earlier, it was not an easy preparation either for my friend Julie, who I would be running with. Julie was now suffering wellbeing issues herself as she dealt with some major changes in her home and work life. Like me, she felt under-prepared and had only managed one 15-mile run in her preparation.

One thing I personally crave when I am struggling in the stormy seas of a period of anxiety is a bit of certainty about what lies ahead; something stable to hang on to. With a company-organised overseas adventure race you at least have a fixed itinerary and pre-booked hotels, even if it can all go pear-shaped as had happened on my previous two trips. On this trip we were a group of 16 friends, all making our own decisions about flights, airport transfers and accommodation, and as the time grew closer our social media feeds pinged endlessly with ideas, questions and debate. All perfectly natural of course, but when you are insecure in your own mind it just added an extra layer of stress. Fortunately one of our number, Richard, brought a measure of control to the situation, organising an early morning pick-up for those travelling from Birmingham airport, and also booking a pre-race pasta meal in the centre of Venice for us all, as we would be spread widely across the city.

Another issue causing some concern for a few of our travelling party was their race registration status. Originally the organisers had requested that overseas competitors should provide a medical certificate, signed by a doctor, to say that they were fit to compete. This, of course, would have incurred some expense, so they eventually relented and said that proof of affiliated membership of your national athletic association, in our case England Athletics, would suffice. On our personal registration pages, the organisers used a traffic light system to indicate our current status. For most of us, including myself, the green light gave us the reassurance we needed but, for a few, and that included Julie, red or amber was showing, despite repeated attempts to email the required proof. There were language barrier issues and, disconcertingly, the advice was that you shouldn't travel to Venice if your traffic light was not green. However, at the 11th hour, the organisers again relented and said outstanding issues would be sorted at registration. What a relief; anxiety sucks.

* * *

The greatest antidote to anxiety is action, so it was a great relief when departure day finally arrived and I could stop worrying about things, most of which were never likely to happen anyway, and just go with the flow. The day started with a flurry of running activity – week six of the couch to 5k programme I was running for our council at our local athletics track – followed by a very wet session with my own Crabbs Cross Chasers group, before picking Julie up and driving us down to a small hotel at Gatwick, from where our flight to Venice left very early the next morning. Once in Venice we would be staying at the very same hotel that I had stayed at the previous year with Chris, Lynne and Cam; this time I was hoping the water levels would be a lot lower.

All went smoothly with the flight, and Julie and I arrived at Marco Polo airport about an hour before the majority of our party would land on the flight from Birmingham. Some had chosen to spend a few days holidaying in Italy beforehand; others would not arrive until the following morning owing to their work commitments, but soon the rest of our group were reunited in the arrivals hall. The consensus was that we should head first to the race headquarters in St Giuliano Park in Mestre, to sort out any registration issues and to pick up our race packets, before then going to the city and our various accommodation choices. Before long our chief organiser, Richard, had negotiated two minibuses to take us to the park where, happily, all the outstanding registration problems, including Julie's, were quickly resolved. Phew!

A quick tour of the expo, a tram ride into the city itself, a walk to our hotel to check in, some initial sightseeing to St Mark's Square as Julie had never visited the city before, and then a pleasant beer and pizza evening with some of our friends in the shadow of the Rialto bridge followed. This was a name that Julie struggled to commit to memory on the trip, and that would subsequently be forever known as 'the famous bridge'. My nerves were now much more settled, apart from those stomach butterfly tingles when I thought about the marathon just two days ahead.

* * *

In the pre-planning phase of this group trip to belatedly celebrate Mike's birthday there was one issue that I was adamant about – a return visit to the Farfalle parkrun in Padua, on the morning before the marathon. You may remember that the previous year I had run it with Chris and some of my other travel companions, and had set a new age category record of a little over 29 minutes, in a record attendance of just 37 runners. Sadly my bragging to Chris that I was a European record holder lasted only about five months before an Italian gentleman knocked a good two minutes off of my time. Could I claim my record back? There was little doubt in my mind that I had it within me to run such a time but, on a woodland course, with many a tree root waiting to trip me up and, more importantly, with a full marathon just 24 hours away, would it be wise to run 'eyeballs out'? I decided to defer to the new holder but nevertheless to enjoy a more leisurely run around the course. I had kept in touch with Alessandro, the event director, since the previous year, and was slightly disappointed to learn that he wouldn't be there on this occasion as, of all places, he was visiting Oxford, just an hour's drive from my home.

To be fair there was quite a lot of initial enthusiasm from our travelling companions at the idea of a parkrun on foreign soil. However, the reality of discovering that Padua was not actually in Venice but 25 miles away, and that this would necessitate a train and taxi journey and a very early start – and all of this the day before running a full marathon – led to the interest gradually waning.

In the end it was just Julie and I who made the moonlit walk to the railway station, with only street cleaners apparently awake at that unearthly hour, and boarded the near-deserted, early morning Padua train. There was a moment of concern at the taxi rank at Padua station when I asked for us to be taken to Farfalle Park, and was told it was 90 minutes' drive away, but a collaborative Googling effort by several taxi drivers soon had us on our way to the correct destination.

So eager had we been to ensure we had plenty of time to make the start, in case of any unexpected delays, that we arrived in the park an hour early and there wasn't a soul around. We walked a lap of the route on a cool but sunny autumn morning but even with ten minutes to go, there were no more than half a dozen people who looked like runners or volunteers. In contrast to the previous year, when there seemed to be quite a few British marathon runners taking in a parkrun before their big day, this year there were just two others. After a last-minute flurry of activity, and the late donning of some yellow volunteer vests, just 19 of us were set on our way around the four-lap, largely trail, course. Remarkably, about 90 seconds later, another latecomer set off in pursuit of the pack and not only caught up with them, but proceeded to finish in first place!

I ran together with Julie on her first overseas parkrun. It was a chatty but respectable pace as we looped through the woods on a twisting route. Of course, ever being the gentleman, I let Julie out-sprint me to the finish line as we took 16th and 17th respectively out of the eventual 20 competitors, in a time a couple of minutes slower than my previous year's effort. Once again the volunteers opened up the little park cafe and we enjoyed a post-run hot drink before they kindly called us a taxi to take us back to the railway station. Another enriching parkrun experience, taking us back to the camaraderie of the earlier days when numbers were much lower, but as we rode the train back to Venice realisation was dawning that a wholly different, and much more arduous challenge, was now less than 24 hours away.

* * *

As I mentioned previously, Richard had booked a pre-race pasta meal for us all that evening at a restaurant just a short walk from the hotel at which Julie and I were staying. After an afternoon of sightseeing, including a walk out to the finish area which we pledged we would be running through the following day, Julie and I enjoyed a small beer at a bar just outside our chosen restaurant as we waited for our group to gather from their various dwellings across the city.

Finally, Richard led us inside to a cluster of tables holding four to six people at each. Having sat down at one of them with Julie, there was then a good deal of shuffling around as people decided who they wanted to chat with at the meal. Once the merry-go-round had finished, Julie and I ended up alone on a table for four with our backs to the rest of the party. I did suggest that at least if we sat on the far side of the table we could see everyone, but Julie insisted we were fine where we were and could easily turn round to talk to those behind us. When a lady insists, you know that is the end of the story, and so I started to peruse the menu. I was about to get the shock of my life.

A familiar voice to my right.

'Is there room for two more?' I turned. It was Chris and Cam. I just stared.

'And please don't swear, you are live on Facebook,' he went on. I didn't swear, I was speechless. Dumbstruck.

They took their seats opposite us. I turned to Julie and asked, 'Did you know about this?' She gave a knowing smile and, at the same time, a ripple of applause passed through our seated party. OK, so everybody knew about this. This was clearly a cleverly orchestrated plan with Richard being at the heart of it, or, as Chris said, the 'secret squirrel'.

My mind turned back ten minutes. I had followed Richard as we had entered the restaurant. 'We've reserved a table for 18,' he said to the waiter on the door. I immediately thought then that there were only 16 of us; perhaps someone else was joining us. Little did I know.

So just 12 months after we had sat at a restaurant table in this very same city with flood water lapping around our feet, our little family group was back together again, and this time surrounded by some of the best running friends anyone could wish for. Chris and Cam explained that they wanted to surprise me to thank me for the support during some very troubling times with Chris's illness, but I was only being a dad and a grandad. At any other time, we would have cracked open a bottle of red wine, apple juice for Cam, and just enjoyed being back together in a wonderful city that we all loved so much. But, hang on a minute, I had a marathon to run the next morning. Just a small beer to accompany my spaghetti carbonara and lemon meringue tart, and then an early night; time for wine would come later.

* * *

If there was one small crumb of comfort as Julie and I set out on successive very early departures from our hotel, it was that we had been gifted an extra hour of sleep as the clocks had gone back. Nevertheless, it was still a dark moonlit walk that we set out on the following morning. The street cleaners were still keeping busy, but now the near-deserted streets of the previous day were alive with runners clad in their colourful outer layers, and we could hear a mixture of excited and nervous chatter in several languages. This time we walked beyond the railway station, and on to Tronchetto, an artificial lagoon island which basically acts as a car park for the city, and from where our buses to the start would leave. It was there that we bumped into Richard and Adam, who were both signed up for the marathon. Richard had trained diligently and was hoping for a sub-four-hour result. Adam had adopted a more laissez-faire approach; with the coolness of youth, he was going to take on a marathon, not with inadequate mileage under his belt like Julie and me, but with no mileage. None. Zilch. Adam hadn't run for a long time, although he used to be quite a decent runner. He had come along for the social aspects of the trip but thought he might as well run the marathon with the rest of us!

The 40-minute bus ride out to the start in the town of Stra is not one I remember fondly. It was one of those single-decker vehicles designed to accommodate as many passengers as possible, so there was minimal seating but plenty of standing room, with little to hang on to. As the driver flung the bus around tight country lane bends and small-town roundabouts we were being tossed around like rag dolls, occasionally apologising for grabbing a complete stranger inappropriately. On top of that, as everyone who has ever run a long-distance race knows, the further you are away from an accessible toilet the greater the need grows. Once we finally climbed off the bus, the number one priority was to find the portaloos and, mercifully, the queues were fairly short.

The Venice Marathon starts outside the majestic Villa Pisani, a rural, late-baroque palace. After a stomach-settling wander around the stunning gardens, it was time to strip off the outer layers, hand in our kit bags, and make our way to the start. Eight of us from our party had signed up for the full marathon experience, and we gathered together outside the villa for one final group hug before moving on to our respective start corrals which were based on predicted times. The number of your start corral was printed on your race number, and these were being checked by officials before letting you into the appropriate area. Young Adam, perhaps in the expectation that he might actually have done some training, had probably been a little over-optimistic with his time prediction, and had been placed in one of the faster corrals, but he wanted to run the race with Stuart, who like most of us, was in corral number five.

If you have read *Can We Run With You, Grandfather?* you may well remember Stuart. Four years earlier, almost to the day, this well-respected, local running coach, and all-round good guy, had come within minutes of losing his life when the walls of a major artery split apart. He survived, just, but had to learn to walk again after losing much of the muscle in one leg, as a result of lost circulation when its blood supply failed. Little by little Stuart had fought his way back to some level of fitness, and now he was lining up to take on a marathon. Adam had been one of the athletes who had benefitted from Stuart's coaching experience, and now he wanted to repay him by helping him around the marathon route. With a combination of deception and distraction, we managed to smuggle Adam past the eagle-eyed officials. We were ready for the off.

* * *

The pact had been agreed. Julie and I would run this marathon, side-by-side, from the start to finish mats. It would take as long as it took; we wouldn't put ourselves under any time target pressure, although we aimed for a pace that would get us home in around five and a half hours, much the same time as I had achieved in Rome seven years previously. With regard to my fuelling strategy, I had made it through my single 16-mile training run using my flexible gel flasks, so saw no

Wandering the flooded streets of Venice with Cam and Lynne.

The small, but super-friendly, Farfalle parkrun in Padua, running with Chris, with our friend Jayne (in black) just behind.

House front street art in the colourful Chilean port city of Valparaiso.

Fallen and partially buried moai on the slopes of the Rano Raruka volcano which supplied the stone (tuff) from which the vast majority of Easter Island's moai were carved.

Look carefully and you will see the facial features of one of the incomplete moai, lying on its back, high on the outside crater wall of Rano Raruka.

The restored Ahu Tongariki, 15 moai facing the sunset during the winter solstice, just one with its pukao (hat).

The huge volcanic crater of Rano Kau on Easter Island, containing a rainwater lake with floating islands of grass and totora reeds.

Looking out from the clifftops of Orongo, the outer island, Moto Nui, was where the manutara bird would lay its eggs, the quest for which was the objective of the ancient annual contest of Easter Island's Birdman cult.

Our 'exclusive' opening ceremony for the Easter Island races, with the Rapa Nui warrior offering us each a piece of chicken from a carcass baked in the ground.

Crossing the finish line of the Easter Island half-marathon in the rather curious time of two hours, 17 minutes and, erm, 73 seconds??

Colourful rehearsals for the children's winter equinox parade in Cusco, Peru.

Looking down on the city of Cusco from the ancient Incan citadel of Sacsayhuaman.

Machu Picchu, bathed in sunshine.

For those who have trekked or run the Inca Trail, the first sighting of Machu Picchu from the Sun Gate (Intipunku).

PeruRail staff on the train back from Aguas Calientes, the gateway to Machu Picchu, are required to do rather more than just provide refreshments!

It may look as if I am working particularly hard, but I'm just running past some of the hot springs at Furnas. (credit: Dave Gratton)

Each of these mounds is owned by a local restaurant and, below ground, a meal is cooking in the steam.

Taken from the volcanic rim during the half-marathon, this photo shows the massive Sete Cidades crater, with the village nestling within it.

reason why I should risk anything different this time. They could be easily carried in the small pouch around my waist in the early miles of the race when I wouldn't be using them, but then squashed up neatly into the palm of my hand later on. The one big advantage for me though was that it allowed me to take on the gel, little and often. Like many, I have a pretty sensitive stomach, and swallowing a whole sachet of gooey gel every few miles would leave me feeling pretty nauseous. Little and often was the key. So that was it. One gel flask was filled with my favourite isotonic pineapple gel, and another with salted strawberry, hoping that the added electrolytes would hold off any late calf cramping, which had been a feature of my later years' endurance running. As far as water was concerned there were plenty of aid stations, so I would rely on them rather than trying to carry any.

Shortly after half past nine on a warm and sunny morning we were set on our way and quickly settled into a steady pace that we knew would get us home in around five hours if we could sustain it all the way, although this was most unlikely given our haphazard preparation. There was one thought uppermost in my mind: please don't fall over! 2019 was becoming by far my worst year for tripping up during a run, and I was still carrying the recent scars from my tumbles in the Azores. Julie was acutely aware of this too; you may remember that on one of our joint training runs in the build-up to the marathon I had fallen twice in the space of seven miles, and she had had to help me up and dust me down. As we ran along the tarmac road alongside the Brenta River, every time the sole of my shoe scuffed the surface Julie would bark at me to keep my feet up, in the nicest possible way, of course.

All was going so well until we reached the two-mile marker. No, I didn't fall, but despite leaving my final trip to the portaloos at the start until the last possible moment, I was now in urgent need of a repeat visit. Damned marathon nerves. There was no way I could hang on for another 24 miles! Julie patiently waited at the side of the road while I slid down a grassy bank and into some convenient bushes and then we were on our way again. In fact, up until the ten-mile marker we were knocking out a really consistent pace on the largely rural road, which tracked the river to our right. There was, of course, very little crowd support other than when we passed through the small towns of Dolo and Mira, where a handful of spectators would line the pavement and cheer us through with cries of 'bravo'. Without Julie at my side I would have missed so many of the features of these quaint Venetian municipalities. My eyes were firmly focused on the next few yards in front of me as I chanted a silent mantra of 'keep your feet up, don't trip'. In contrast, Julie was taking in all the sights and delights of running on foreign soil, and making sure I didn't miss out.

It was while passing through Oriago that the pace began to slip just a little, with the occasional short walk break of 100 strides before then running again. Let's face it, the Venice Marathon course is probably as flat as you can ever get; the occasional up and down slope but there are no monster hills to stop you in your tracks. We ran on into the small community of Malcontenta, passing the delightful Villa Foscari, a UNESCO World Heritage Site on the opposite bank of the river. How apt that when you reach the point of a marathon where your legs are just beginning to remind you of how far it is, that you should pass through a place called Malcontenta! And it was there that we finally said goodbye to the river that had flowed at our side for most of the first ten miles of the race as our route swung north towards Marghera, where we would reach the halfway point.

While I continued to focus my attention on propelling one foot after the other and staying upright, Julie was able to multitask and keep me informed about how some of the others were progressing. Like most modern-day city marathons, a little chip attached to our race number meant we were being constantly tracked by our supporters waiting to greet us at the end, and messages were going back and forth which Julie was picking up on her phone and watch. How times have changed! Somewhere around our 15-mile point a very disappointing message came through. Our courageous friend Stuart had decided that enough was enough and had pulled out of the race at halfway. On an occasion like this, it does take some bravery to admit that your body can't take any more and to make that tough decision. Stuart HAD completed a half-marathon, and who would have thought that was possible just four years previously? His day would come.

As we ran on towards Mestre, a familiar voice came up behind us. It was Adam. He had been accompanying Stuart and was able to reassure us that the big man was OK but just knew he didn't yet have it within him to double up the distance he had already run. Adam ran with us both for a while and then his younger legs pushed him on ahead.

As we approached the outskirts of Mestre, a much larger conurbation, the route took an unconventional twist when we suddenly found we were running indoors. No blue sky and warm sun above us now but an air-conditioned building which seemed to be a mixture of a shopping mall and a business centre. After half a mile or so we emerged again on to the open road, and the heat was now getting a little oppressive as the sun rose higher. Although we were remaining at a consistent pace when running, some of the walking breaks were getting a little longer. The encouragement of rather more spectators was urging us along, though. At 18 miles we entered the outskirts of San Giuliano Park, the race headquarters where we had registered just a few days before. The direction markers took us on a meandering route around the park, a little more undulating than most of the roads we had run, but nothing too challenging. It was there that Julie demonstrated another one of her capabilities, other than the constant chatter and encouragement: her ability to spot an official race photographer at a distance. I am quite sure that without her at my side, most of my photographs would have had me staring grimly at the ground a few feet in front of me. With my early warning system in place, and with photographers becoming more and more prolific as we entered the race's final stages, I ended up with a great collection of happy, waving pictures which perhaps didn't really reflect my inner feelings for much of the race.

As we left the park we had just over six miles to go, and within a few minutes we were running up gentle ramps to get on to the Ponte della Libertà – the two-and-a-half-mile-long Liberty Bridge that links the mainland to the lagoon islands and historical centre of Venice. As soon as we reached the road on the bridge, we could see our goal – the outline of Venice on the horizon, dominated by the Campanile bell tower in St Mark's Square. Julie suggested a modification of our run-walk strategy as we were both still feeling fairly strong: every time we reached a mile marker, we would walk for 400 metres, measured by our watches, and then run to the next mile marker. It worked well. Once or twice a run phase was briefly interrupted by an aid station where I could gulp down some more water. My little-by-little gel approach was working well for me, and my sometimes temperamental stomach was as settled as it has ever been at this stage of a marathon. Julie, with a hardier constitution, was happy to eat whatever was on offer at the aid stations to keep her going.

Almost before we knew it, we were off the bridge and into a rather isolated tour of the Venetian dockyards at the western end of the island, with huge cruise liners towering above us. It was there that we met up again with Adam at an aid station. He was really struggling to keep any sort of momentum going, paying the price for his total lack of training but, as ever, he had a cheerful disposition and the knowledge that he would get to the end come what may. As we finally swung to the east, and followed the narrow footpath that ran alongside the channel that separated the main island from the island of Giudecca, a trip could have had a watery ending. Julie continued to remind me to keep my feet up on the uneven, brick surface, but finishing was now a certainty for us both, barring something absolutely catastrophic.

By this stage of many of my marathons, I would normally have hit the dreaded 'wall'. This would see me interspersing periods of walking with a painful hobbling run due to the intense calf cramps. Curiously, this pain would disappear once I had passed the 26-mile marker, and the final, triumphant 385 yards to the finish line would be a breeze. Maybe it was our decision to just back off the pace a little in that crucial half-marathon phase between ten and 23 miles; maybe the salted gels were keeping my cramps at bay. Whatever it was, I now knew we would not only finish, but we would also run the final mile and a half non-stop. When we rounded the corner alongside the Santa Maria della Salute basilica, we enjoyed an experience denied to almost all visitors to Venice; we crossed the Grand Canal on the slightly wobbly pontoon bridge that is erected each year for the marathon weekend, and then dismantled again. Julie was still spotting race photographers with an uncanny knowhow, and our smiles were ever broader.

As we reached the two towering granite columns that overlook the entrance to St Mark's Square, the route swung left as we headed for a circuit of the square itself. I loved this section. Crowds were six deep behind the steel barriers that separated them from the runners. Children leant over the fences to high-five the passing athletes and orchestras played beneath the facades of some of the city's finest restaurants. Julie was less enthusiastic about this bit as, for a short time, we had turned our backs on the finish line and were running away from it. This didn't stop her spotting another photographer though, momentarily bringing us to a halt so as not to miss another picture opportunity.

Soon we were out of the square, back on track towards the finish. The Doge's Palace, the Bridge of Sighs. Normally passing over the canal inlets meant crossing a small bridge with steps either side. Out of consideration for our legs, the Italian military had laid ramps over the steps which can be quite daunting for tired limbs, but we ran every one. As we entered the final mile we heard shouts of support from our right; it was Chris and Cam.

A short time later saw more raucous cheering, this time from the left, as we passed the bulk of our supporting group and some of our faster runners, enjoying a beer on the waterfront. As the finish line came in sight, Julie grabbed my hand and, arms aloft, we crossed together just as we said we would. Mission accomplished and, in contrast to the previous year's race, all without getting our feet wet once.

* * *

My time was around ten minutes slower than my previous marathon in Rome. It was almost two hours slower than my lifetime personal best but, if you are into comparing times, this run was over two hours faster than my marathon in the Sahara, when I was probably at the peak of my fitness. Times don't define a marathon, and nothing quite compares to that feeling of accomplishment that surges through your body as you cross the line, whatever the last 26 and a bit miles had thrown at you.

If this was to be my final full marathon, and the jury remains out on that one, I could not have wished to have run it with a more supportive friend than Julie. The plan had worked; Julie talked all the way through, and I listened! Once we had posed for our official finisher photos, brandishing our medals, we picked up a goody bag which, mercifully, included a can of beer. We met up with Chris and Cam, and then with the rest of our chums at the bar alongside the finishing straight. There was a feeling of great celebration in the air, matched only by the sizes of our beer mugs. Richard had achieved his target of going below four hours, Stuart was upbeat with his performance and vowed that he had unfinished business with the course, and Adam, despite zero preparation, still had a marathon medal around his neck, having finished just a few minutes behind Julie and myself. Everybody else had achieved what they had set out to, and it was a group trip nobody wanted to end. Sadly most people were going home the following morning so, after a return to our respective hotels for a shower and a snooze, we all enjoyed one final triumphant meal together that evening and, this time, the wine really did flow.

As Julie had never visited Venice before, I had booked an extra night at the hotel after the marathon, so at least we could do some sightseeing of such a fabulous city and, being aware of my plans, Chris and Cam had arranged the same for their undercover operation. So as not to risk spoiling the surprise, they had booked a different hotel close to ours, but we were all able to spend a relaxing and laughter-filled day and a half, enjoying all that Venice had to offer in the way of food, drink and, of course, an obligatory gondola cruise which took us under 'the famous bridge'.

Chapter 7

Trails, trips and trophies

THE PACE of the islands challenge was now becoming quite relentless. With less than four weeks between my marathon in Venice and my first race in Cyprus it was time to tweak the training, shifting the emphasis from distance to hills. Having run the Cyprus event three years previously, for once I knew what was coming. But you know me. Settle me down in an armchair at home with a glass of red wine at my side and I will start to browse for new challenges. Even during this short time interval, I managed to rope myself in for two more foreign adventures.

The first of these was a series of half-marathons in European cities, collectively called the Superhalfs. The cities in question were Cardiff, Copenhagen, Lisbon, Prague and Valencia, and the challenge was to complete each of these within a 36-month period to be inducted into their SuperRunner Hall of Fame. It sounded fun; an opportunity to travel to some European cities for a long weekend with a bit of running thrown in. You may remember that Clare and I had already signed up for the Prague half-marathon in March 2020, as a European reunion with our American friends Liz, Cathy and Drew, from the Easter Island trip. Flights and hotel were already arranged, so that was one in the bag already. Cardiff was only a two-hour drive from my front door and the October 2020 date slotted nicely into my plans, so I quickly secured a spot in that race as well. That left me two years to complete the other three. I had taken part in a city running tour in Copenhagen in 2013, on my way to the Polar Circle half-marathon in Greenland, but I had never raced there, and Valencia and Lisbon would be new cities for me. Exciting.

The other temptation that I completely failed to resist was a new offering from my friends at Albatros Adventure Marathons. I had already experienced four amazing races with them in Jordan, South Africa, Greenland and Myanmar and knew that I could expect a very demanding run, but with superb organisational support. This time they dangled the carrot of a half-marathon in an active volcanic zone in north-east Iceland. Another island, another volcano. What was it with volcanoes? Until I had stared in awe into the massive rain-filled crater of Rano Kau on Easter Island just a few months previously, I don't think I had really appreciated the extent of our planet's true power when it chooses to unleash it. And even more recently the slopes of the Sete Cidades volcanic complex in the Azores had brought me to the brink of exhaustion, saved only by the uplift that the jaw-dropping beauty of these incredible natural phenomena brings, to me at least. Was I really considering another run up and around the rim of a volcano? I signed up before I could question myself any further.

* * *

But now Cyprus beckoned. You may have noticed that when it comes to my overseas running adventures I never go back to the same place twice, no matter how enjoyable the event was. Life is short and I want to experience as many different parts of our world as possible while I still can. Yes, I had returned to Venice, but that was because injury stopped me from running the marathon the first time round. In contrast, at home in the UK, there are local races that I usually sign up for year after year. The Not The Roman IX in Stratford-upon-Avon is traditionally my first race of the year; June would not be the same without taking on the massive hill towards the end of the Timberhonger 10km, part of the Bromsgrove summer festival, and the autumn Alcester 10km was always a fabulous occasion with most of the town's people turning out to support. So why return to Cyprus when I had completed the event three years previously?

Multiple reasons really, but primarily the format. At an age when single-day marathons and beyond were becoming less attractive, and enjoyment was still my number one reason for running, the mix of shorter and longer distances, road and trail, and the satisfaction of pushing yourself hard in a competitive environment but still leaving enough in the tank for the days to come were all part of the appeal. My recent four-race experiences in the Azores had only served to enhance this feeling. The late-November date was also a draw. Like many, my mood can be affected by the seasons. The prospect of a week of sunshine and warmth, albeit not guaranteed, was appealing, particularly at a time of year when the hours of daylight would be getting shorter, and with the prospect of a long winter ahead. The late-autumn break had certainly given me a massive boost when I ran the event three years previously.

This time I would have a new travelling companion: Paul. Having only started running about five years previously, once he was in his 50s, Paul had already progressed to marathons and was looking for new challenges. He and his wife Cheryl had often been part of the running groups I led, and both were regular parkrunners. I remembered that when I ran the Cyprus event in 2016, and came home with a DVD of the highlights, Paul asked to see it and said that it was the type of occasion that he would love to take part in one day as his overseas race debut. Well, that day had arrived. Cheryl had given him time off for good behaviour, or that is what Paul said anyway. Paul always liked to blame me every time he stepped up a gear with his running adventures but, if truth be told, the guy needed little encouragement. Personality-wise we were chalk and cheese. I have always been rather introverted until I get to know someone well, whereas Paul can chatter at length to anyone and everyone, but when it came to running we were roughly of an equal standard and we were both very much in favour of an after-run pint or two. It had all the makings of a good week.

* * *

Although we would room and run together, we had made separate travel arrangements. Paul is a self-employed window cleaner and was keen to get back to work on the Monday after the final race. That meant missing the celebration dinner and awards ceremony, which he didn't think he would be in contention for anyway, but it had the benefit of allowing him to take advantage of a great-priced flight to and from Birmingham. I, on the other hand, had really enjoyed the dinner on my previous visit and, although I had finished well out of the reckoning for silverware back then, I was now in a higher age category and, well, who knows? This did mean that there was no Birmingham flight on the day I planned to travel back, so I settled once more for Gatwick, with an overnight stay before the early morning outbound flight at the same hotel I had stayed in with Julie before our Venice trip.

If you have followed my story from the very beginning you will be aware that, all too often, a last-minute medical hitch can often throw a spanner in the works of my plans. Why this is, I have no idea. My underlying anxiety issues do mean that I tend to get quite nervous in the build-up to a foreign trip, particularly if I am travelling alone; maybe this impacts my immune system? Who knows? In any case, this trip was about to begin with its own mini-drama.

Following the marathon I had recovered quickly, and my training for Cyprus, which included a lot of hill work, had gone as well as I possibly could have expected. The only slight concern was an unusual tummy and back pain in the final 36 hours before leaving home. No sickness or diarrhoea; just a sensation that didn't feel quite right. I brushed it off as nerves and set off for the drive down to Gatwick. This was a journey I would make on a fairly regular basis, when I travelled down to Sussex to visit family. Normally I would expect to make the trip in one go without any comfort breaks. This time I had to make two very necessary service station visits, and not for fuel. It was becoming clear that the mystery tummy pains were likely due to a urinary tract infection, and that would probably need a course of antibiotics to sort out. Yet there I was, heading away from my GP who could have provided them for me.

Needless to say, my overnight stay in the hotel was interrupted on numerous occasions by visits to the bathroom, and when I arrived at the airport early the next morning the very first place I headed to was the pharmacy. Unable to provide what I really needed because of the lack of a prescription, the pharmacist was able to offer some citrate sachets which he hoped might relieve some of the symptoms; three sachets a day, dissolved in water, for two days. With the hope that there may be some medical help associated with the race series once I reached Cyprus, I sat down to read the information leaflet that came with the powders. 'Not suitable for men or children' it said at the very beginning!

I returned to the pharmacist but he assured me there would be no unwanted side effects, and I dissolved my first sachet in a glass of water on the flight out.

* * *

It was comforting to arrive at a hotel I was familiar with, although compared to three years previously the room we had been allocated was in a completely different part of what is a vast complex. Paul's flight, which was supposed to arrive only an hour behind mine, was delayed and by the time his airport transfer dropped him off at the hotel it was already dark. In the meantime I had managed to get registered and spoken to the race organisers about seeing a doctor. While they could provide physiotherapy, sports massage and first aid, prescription medicines were not within their remit so I was directed to the hotel reception for advice. There I was told that I could visit a medical centre in the town of Paphos the following morning, so the magic powders would have to see me through to then, although there were already signs that the symptoms were relenting a little bit.

Once Paul had registered, we enjoyed a nice buffet dinner at the hotel followed by a couple of chatty pints of the local brew. There was no doubting that Paul was buzzing and really up for the running adventures ahead.

* * *

The following morning was a mix of good and bad for me. On the plus side I had only needed to get up once during the night to visit the bathroom. By breakfast time, sachet number four had been consumed and the signs were all moving in the right direction. I decided that I would see how the first, relatively short, race went before seeking further medical help, but then another potential problem popped its head over the parapet.

Paul had gone out for an exploratory walk around the hotel. I decided that I would make a trip over to the supermarket across the road to bulk buy some bottled water to see me through the next few days, but then experienced that sinking feeling in the pit of your stomach when you realise your credit card is not where you expected it to be. I undertook a frantic, but fruitless, search of all the pockets and bags where it might be hiding. I'd last used the card in the hotel bar the previous evening – could I have dropped it there? If I had, hopefully an honest person finding it would have handed it in, but a check with the hotel reception drew a blank. I feared the worst. I sat outside in the warm sunshine and made the call to the lost and stolen cards hotline of my bank. When they told me that no further transactions had been made on the card, the relief hissed out of me. There were too many unwanted distractions on this trip; I just wanted to get the running started.

* * *

So eager were Paul and I to get the show on the road that we were sitting in the front row of the large hall that was hosting the pre-event briefing at least ten minutes before anybody else arrived. Just as it had been three years previously, the briefing was led by Mike, who gave us a comprehensive description of each of the four stages, and Yiota from Arena Sports, who outlined the history of an event that was now in its 15th year. There were people there who had run all, or most, of them. As expected, the format was the same as three years previously, with just a few minor tweaks to the routes because of road and building works: a 6km time trial, where the runners are set off individually at ten-second intervals, an 11km uphill race, a trail half-marathon, and finishing with the road 10km around Paphos itself. When the meeting broke up there would be just over an hour before the first runner was set on their way.

* * *

The runners milled about in the afternoon sunshine on the beach promenade outside of our hotel, many grabbing a last-minute snack or gulping down some water. For me, it was good to see some familiar faces among them. I greeted Nigel, the Welshman I had roomed with back in 2016, and there were several people there from the Azores trip just a couple of months previously, both among the runners and from Mike's team of eager helpers. And, as before, there was a strong British military presence with multiple teams from both the army and the RAF.

Mike would set each of us off at the appropriate time, and with well over 250 runners signed up many would be finished before others had even started. There was no seeding according to ability; you were simply launched on your way in the order of the race number pinned to the front of your vest. I was number 34, and Paul was 35, so at least we didn't have to wait around for too long once the action got under way. As we edged towards the front of the queue we wished each other well on the challenges that lay ahead. We had agreed to just run our own races, enjoy the experience, and hopefully come away with finisher medal's to show off to those at home.

Mike called me forward to the start line. Five, four, three, two, one, go. I sped off along the flat promenade to encouraging shouts of support from a sizeable crowd lining the route. Pretty soon, the path swung to the right and started to climb, circling back to the front of the hotel and taking a route through the extensive car parks. It was at this point that Paul caught up with me, and then as we reached the first downhill stretch when we turned on to the main road Paul slowly started to pull away. I maybe could have kept up with him, but I was intently monitoring my body to see if it was sending me any painful warning signs. So far, so good.

Soon we were taking a series of turns, towards, and then away from, the setting sun, which was now quite low in the sky and quite an uncomfortable distraction when we were heading straight towards it. Memories of the route were flooding back as I reached each turn and, little by little, my confidence was growing and I could gradually pick up the pace. There was field upon field of banana plants, the bunches of fruit protected inside bright blue plastic bags, that apparently also improve the speed of ripening. On quite a regular basis a much faster runner would come hammering past me, probably having started many minutes behind. Much more rarely I caught up with, and overtook, someone with a lower race number than mine; you never quite know how you are performing with the time trial format. I seemed to be engaged in a seesaw battle with another elderly gentleman who had a race number just a few higher than mine. I wondered whether we were in the same age category. While he could run at a faster pace than me, he was adopting a run-walk strategy, so I would go back past him whenever he was in a walk phase.

As we reached the five-kilometre point we passed very close to the final finishing area which was alive with crowd noise and loudspeaker commentary, but we had one more loop of first running away from the coast and then back towards it to go. It was during this loop that I caught up again with Paul. He was having a little trouble with his breathing in the unaccustomed, warm sunshine, and was taking a little puff on his inhaler. He reassured me he was OK and I pressed on towards the finish, in the company of my unknown racing nemesis, whom I subsequently discovered to be a Swedish man called Thomas. We ran side-by-side for the final kilometre and now I really was picking up the pace as Thomas had dispensed with his walk breaks. I knew there was a twist in the tail of this race, with the final 100 metres up a steep loose shingle bank but, try as I might, Thomas just pipped me by a short head as we crossed the line.

Was I disappointed? Not a bit of it. As I struggled to regain my breath, I knew that whatever had been going on health-wise over the past few days was not going to stop me. I was pain-free, had got faster the further the race went, and subsequently found that I was 16 seconds quicker than I had been three years earlier. Paul finished only a few seconds behind me, and we celebrated our 'one down, three to go' achievements with the customary Cyprus Challenge finish line selection of water, fresh fruit and bags of raisins. Looking out to sea, as the sun slid slowly towards the horizon, lay the beached wreck of the *Edro III*. Without doubt the hull was a lot rustier than it had been three years previously.

After dinner that evening, washed down with a couple of celebratory beers, Paul and I went to the race registration area in the hotel to check the day's official results. To my surprise, I had recorded the fastest time in my 70–74-year-old age group. Thomas was actually in the age group just below. If there is one advantage of getting older it is that you are running against fewer and fewer rivals. I am certainly no speedster and usually struggle to get into the top three in my age category at my local parkrun. The prospect that I might be in for an age category prize just upped the pressure a tiny bit and, on looking a little closer at the results, I saw there were just five others in my age group. Two of these had been significantly slower, but the remaining three looked very evenly matched, at least on the first flat route. I'm not a particularly competitive person, but something was stirring deep inside.

* * *

By the time my alarm clock sounded at 6.30am the following day, all six sachets of my citrate powder had been consumed and, mercifully, I was feeling a whole lot better. This was undoubtedly good news. While the distance of the second run of the challenge was just under double the length of the previous day's course, we were about to encounter a wholly different beast. Having the benefit of having run the route before, I had urged Paul to include as many hills as possible in his build-up training programme. In the space of 11 kilometres we would be climbing over 2,200 feet (670 metres), and this would be relentless from the start to the finish line, apart from one joyous half-mile section just beyond the halfway point. Conditions underfoot would also be very testing, particularly in the early miles, with a loose and rocky surface to contend with.

We gathered at the start on the clifftops looking out over Lara Bay, at the beginning of the Akamas national park. Even at just after nine o'clock in the morning the sun was already feeling strong on our backs and the sky was pretty cloudless. As had happened three years before, the slowest runners from the previous day's time trial were set on their way some 20 minutes before the main pack and began the zig-zag up the hillside route, climbing up above our heads.

At 9.30am the rest of us were set on our way. Again, Paul and I would just run our own races according to how we felt. My initial goal was to reach the first water station at around four kilometres, next to some old farm buildings, and I was inwardly quite pleased with how much of it I was running, taking only the very occasional short walk break on some of the steeper sections, my hands clamped to the front of my thighs to drive up them. I am a pretty silent runner, apart from the rasping of my breathing on the tougher slopes. Paul, on the other hand, is one of those people who will chat to anyone and everyone, just as Julie had been in Venice. We were seesawing in position as we climbed, and I could hear him as he came up behind me, chatting to a runner from one of the all-female army teams, and proudly telling me that he was trying to persuade her to read my books, as he swept past.

I took a good drink on board at the old barn, having decided not to carry water with me on a relatively short route, and not too long afterwards I was taking in the delights of the one downhill section on a tarmac road, for a whole five or six minutes. Once you have reached the river at the bottom of the slope the route then begins to climb again out of the valley. Having said that, it was at this point that some of the surrounding geological features became quite mind-boggling; colourful rock layering and exquisitely sculpted lava formations – there is nothing like the wonders of nature to take your mind off any racing aches and pains. After another water station at around eight kilometres, I again found myself part of a small group of runners that included Paul, and this time our final destination, the picturesque village of Pano Arodes, was within view, although it was perched on top of a rather imposing hill. The final half mile of the route climbed up through the village, on a gradient as steep as anything during the stage, but at least now we had the urgings of the villagers to encourage us to the top. A tight U-turn, an emboldening cheer from Mike, and there before us was the finish arch in the square of the village's 18th-century church. Two stages down, two to go.

* * *

One of the most fascinating aspects of these multi-day race challenges, for me at least, was managing your personal discipline. Here we were in warm November Mediterranean sunshine, while people at home were more than likely shivering. To all intents and purposes we were on holiday, and the temptation to have a few extra glasses of cold beer, a bottle of wine, or extra helpings from the dessert trolley was all too great. But there were also four challenging races to complete on four successive days. Where do you strike the balance? I'm not even going to try and persuade you that I became teetotal for those days, and adopted the dietary habits of a first-rate nutritionist, but finding the right balance can be a test.

We were back at our hotel by early afternoon, and it would have been rude not to celebrate with Paul our ongoing success with a glass or two of beer in the sunshine. We had finished within a handful of seconds of each other, and personally I was once again delighted to have beaten my 2016 time, on the identical route, by more than three minutes. All was going well, and judging by his social media posts Paul was loving every minute. If there was to be a slight 'coming down to earth moment' it came on our post-dinner visit to the official results board. As pleased as I had been with my run and time, one of my age category opponents, a Dutchman called Jean, had finished over five minutes in front of me. This had dropped me down to second in my age category, and cumulatively, I was now nearly two and a half minutes behind. As I have said, I am not a naturally competitive being, but that inner stirring just moved up a notch.

* * *

Race three, and once again the sun shone down on us rather more effectively than was comfortable to run a trail half-marathon in. As on my previous visit three years earlier, we started in the village of Neo Chorio, although construction work in the village square meant that we were no longer set on our way to the sound of church bells. Instead we started on a narrow street that climbed steeply out of the village for over half a mile; this was not exactly welcomed by my quads which were still grumbling from the previous day's exertions. I had spotted my nemesis, Jean, briefly as we had joined the long queues for the portaloos before the start, but then lost him in the crowds and had no idea whether he had got off the line in front of or behind me. After the initial sapping ascent the gradient eased off a little, although it was still in an upward direction as we passed alongside olive fields. At least at this stage there was tarmac beneath our feet and running was still continuous, but soon the rocky underfoot conditions returned, the banks at the side of the trail deepened, and the gradient became that much more brutal. Time for a few walk breaks again.

When we reached the first aid station at around four kilometres, I felt a surge of elation. I knew what was coming. The climbing, for now, was done and the next five kilometres was entirely downhill. Just imagine – an entirely downhill parkrun. We were now over 1,000 feet above sea level, and far below us we could see the shimmering Mediterranean. The wide trail down had numerous switchback bends, with steep, sometimes unprotected drops at the side, so a degree of caution was needed to avoid losing control on the steeper parts. I took on a good drink of water even though the hydration pack on my back was still almost full. The heat from the sun was noticeably increasing, and I wanted to save as much water as I could for the latter stages of the race in the midday heat. I set off again.

My joy was short-lived. Within a few hundred yards of the aid station I was flat on my face, eating the dirt of the trail. Yet again I had tripped. I pulled myself into a sitting position to examine the damage; the usual bloody abrasions on knees, elbows and palms but, luckily, I had avoided any facial cuts or bruises. A passing runner handed me a water-soaked sponge he had picked up at the drink stop and I was able to wash the worst of the grit out of the bleeding wounds. Paul came by but I reassured him I would be fine and urged him on his way, and then I gingerly picked myself up and carried on running.

It was a somewhat surreal experience as I spent almost all of the descent running alone, with no other runners in sight. Aside from another aid station where I exchanged one blood-stained sponge for a clean one, I saw nobody. I could accept that I was not making ground on those already ahead of me but I was a little surprised that there was nobody coming from behind to overtake. I was running with a degree of caution; not so much because the still bleeding wounds were causing any more than an irksome soreness, but more because I just didn't want to risk falling for a second time. I even began to doubt that I was still on the correct track and had somehow strayed off-route, but the trail really was a one-way street, and any deviation from it would have found you in some very uncomfortably steep surroundings. It was only in the final half a kilometre of the descent that a young man came racing past me at such a pace that I was left wondering why he had remained behind me for so long; perhaps he wasn't even part of our race.

As I approached the end of the descent, and was ready to make the left turn that would take us on to the coastal path towards the finish, I spotted in the distance our official photographer, Kevin, standing on the roof of a hardtop jeep, with camera and long lens in hand. It was a momentary lapse of concentration. Taking my eyes, just for that moment, off the rocky trail underfoot, I rolled my right ankle with a ferocity that made me yell out loud like a Premier League footballer eager to ensure the referee hadn't missed a foul. I somehow managed to keep myself upright as I wildly lurched off balance, but my immediate thought was that this could be a race-ending injury.

Aren't ankle ligaments incredible? I ground to a halt and gently began to flex my right foot in several directions but the pain was dull and not really worse with any particular direction of the foot. I tentatively tried putting more weight on the foot; again, a dull ache but no acute pain. I could already begin to feel the joint swelling, but I could bear weight without pain, so decided to press on and see how it went. Within a few hundred yards I became aware that the right-hand side of my vest and shorts were becoming increasingly wet. I stopped again only to discover that the bite valve on the end of the drinking tube of my hydration pack was no longer in place, and most of the water I was carrying had siphoned out; a deja vu moment of something that had happened to me in Myanmar several years earlier. It had probably happened during my wild cavorting to regain my balance after the ankle roll but there was no way I was going to go back to look for it; most of the water had already escaped anyway. I was yet to reach the halfway point of this particular stage and, fair to say, it was not going well.

At least I was now down to sea level, or at least clifftop above the sea level. That didn't mean the route was flat though; the coastal trail dipped and climbed repeatedly as it wound around various bays and coves and, every now and again, a hired quad bike would come zooming past, throwing up a huge cloud of sand that hung in the air for an age. I'd be lying if I didn't admit that I was finding this stage a real struggle; while not painful, my ankle was throbbing and the loss of my water supply was becoming a problem as the temperature continued to climb. I was having to introduce more walk intervals than I would have hoped for and it was clear that, unlike on the two previous days, I was not going to better the time I had run on this route three years previously. Nevertheless, it's character-building moments like this that you look back on with pride in the future, and that was what was keeping me going.

With just under a mile to go the road dropped down towards beach level and the finishing arch was in sight, although just that little bit further away than three years previously to compensate for the shifted start. The final stretch in soft beach sand was tough on the calves but I was now endowed with that extra package of energy that always comes into play when you can sense the finish. Paul was waiting to greet me; he had had a great run and had finished ten minutes in front of me. I quaffed a huge amount of water and then made my way to the first aid ambulance to get the fall wounds cleaned up and dressed, and a quick check of the ankle to confirm that it was still good to go for just one more run.

* * *

Although I was initially feeling a bit deflated with my performance, Paul, and the mood-lifting effects of a couple more pints of cold beer, soon had me smiling again. Paul was buzzing and together we plotted a return visit in 2020, only this time we would persuade a few of our local parkrunners to join us and form a team. The post-dinner trip to the official results posting also brought some joy. Of the five other runners in my age group who had originally started out only three were still running, and I was astonished to see that I had led the trio home in the half-marathon, although my two friendly foes finished within a minute of me. Paul now had a lead of over nine minutes on me overall but, in terms of the age category, although I was still second, I had narrowed Jean's lead to a minute and a quarter. Could I claw that back on the final road 10km? My restrained competitive instincts were stirring again.

* * *

With an 8am start to the 10km race, as most of it took place along a very busy seafront in a resort city, I was up bright and early. After a light breakfast I strapped up my still-throbbing ankle and took a potentially unwise equine dose of ibuprofen to dull the discomfort. Buses dropped us off at the start and finish area in the shadow of the imposing Paphos Castle, overlooking the western end of the city's harbour. Memories of three years ago came flooding back. Although the start and finish of the race would remain as before, major works on one of the city's main roads meant a long coastal road out and back in the middle section of the race.

As we were called forward for the start, I found myself edging slightly further ahead than I might usually have done. Paul, knowing that I was on something of a secret mission, was happy to hang back and just enjoy the occasion, still relishing his success of the previous day, although bearing some of the consequences in his legs. The klaxon sounded and we were away. I quickly settled into quite a brisk pace for me; these days the first mile is usually about loosening up the joints. I looked around for any sign of Jean but couldn't spot him. There were considerably more runners on this leg. As with the trail half-marathon on the previous day, it was possible to enter it as a one-off event rather than as part of the whole four-race series. Not many people had taken up the offer of the half-marathon, but numbers now were definitely boosted by holidaymakers eager to add a burst of vigorous exercise to their break.

After a circuit around the main part of the town we rejoined the coastal road, still relatively quiet at that time of the morning but with frequent barriers keeping the runners and tourists apart. A glance at my watch showed that I was running at quicker than nine minutes per mile, which was pretty fast for me at this stage of my career. Still no sighting of Jean. Was he going even faster?

A little beyond the halfway point, we swung around a roundabout and started to head back towards the city, and the castle finish. Now we could see those still heading outwards on the other side of the road. After a few minutes I spotted Paul, happily chatting away as ever to those around him, and we exchanged thumbs up. A short time later I saw Jean, and there was that momentary relief as I realised he was several minutes behind me. But this was no time to relax. Maybe he was saving himself for a really hard effort in the final miles.

I pushed on. I was holding the pace that my legs hadn't really been accustomed to for quite some time, but it was getting harder. And then I was back in among the seaside cafes, the whiff of cooked breakfasts in the air, ripples of applause coming from those sitting at the outside tables. The fort came into view, a final surge to the sounds of vibrant music and an excited commentator over the PA, and the line was crossed: the challenge was complete. Fifty-five minutes exactly; my fastest 10km time for several years and, as other runners of whatever pace will recognise, at that particular moment I felt invincible.

With the medal hanging round my neck and the challenge certificate in my hand, I joined the back of the free beer queue, one of the many highlights of this fabulous race series. A few minutes later Paul crossed the line and joined the celebrations, and he was followed shortly after by Jean, my unknowing adversary. Although my pumped-up performance had beaten Paul fairly and squarely on the day, he still held the upper hand on me for the overall series by a margin of just under two minutes, so we both had reasons to celebrate. We may even have rejoined the free beer queue a couple more times before the barrels ran out.

* * *

The awards ceremony and dinner that evening was a rare excursion for me into the realms of silverware. Paul was already on his travels home, although his hopes of getting straight back down to his window cleaning were to be dashed by typical British November rainstorms.

I was first called to the stage to be presented with a trophy for being the overall winner for my M70 age category to raucous applause, particularly from the table behind where I sat, occupied by two teams from RAF Cranwell. I had befriended one of the guys in the previous couple of days, as he was also a veteran of a recent Marathon des Sables and, as I have said before, this engenders a massive mutual respect between what were, previously, complete strangers.

A short time later I was called forward once again, to the same boisterous reception, to collect another trophy for my age group win in the half-marathon. There was also another trophy on offer for the 10km race but, despite my unexpected performance, this was taken by a British runner who had only entered this individual race, and he won it in a time that I hadn't run for over 20 years, so hats off to him.

So forgive me for my smug self-satisfaction. My walls at home are adorned with dozens of medals for finishing races, at home or abroad. Podium finishes and silverware, however, were a very rare beast for a bang average runner, and if I needed any further evidence of that, if I had run this same race series in the M75 age category, I would have finished third! In the words of the oft-used cliche in the sporting world, 'you can only beat what is in front of you'!

Chapter 8

Rum on the run

AFTER THREE consecutive months of travelling and enjoying races from 5km to full marathon, on and off road, December 2019 offered the opportunity to unwind a little, enjoy the festivities with family, and just keep the running ticking over as all the hard training was done. Next on the horizon, early in the new year, was the Bermuda Triangle adventure, the final three events of my islands challenge.

As I mentioned previously, Clare would once again be joining me on this trip, with husband Bill's blessing, as the flight was rather too long for his liking. It was also an opportunity for a reunion with some of the American friends we had made on Easter Island. Unfortunately Catharine had had to drop out because of work commitments, but Liz would still be there, as well as Drew, who would be bringing along his mum Lynn.

My mood of calm anticipation of this new and exciting challenge was somewhat disrupted when an unexpected letter arrived on my doormat just a few days before Christmas. In the UK, once you are of a certain age, you are invited every couple of years to take part in a free screening programme for bowel cancer. A test kit is sent to you in the post, you collect a tiny sample of faeces and return it in a sealed container and, all being well, you receive a letter a few days later giving you the all-clear. I had done this on several occasions in the past and, although the sample collection test kit had been a little different this time, I had absolutely no cause to believe that the outcome would be any different as I opened the NHS envelope.

I was wrong. This time the letter said that further tests were needed and recommended that I undertake a colonoscopy procedure. While reassuring me that nine out of ten people who have a colonoscopy do not have bowel cancer, I didn't want to dwell on the fact that it meant ten per cent do, and that this was going to cast something of a shadow over Christmas. But it was time to pull the big boy pants up! If it hadn't been for the letter there was not the slightest indication that anything was amiss and, if the news were to be on the darker side, then at least the screening system had done its job and, hopefully, interventions at an earlier stage would lead to a more positive outcome.

There were two hospital appointments involved; the first would take place just a couple of days before we were due to fly out to Bermuda, and would describe what the procedure comprised, answer any questions that I may have, and then get my informed consent to go ahead. Once this had been agreed, there was then the explanation of what I needed to do to prepare myself beforehand, so that 'nothing' got in the way of the little camera that would be travelling through my large intestine, if you know what I mean. The colonoscopy procedure itself was due to take place about ten days after I returned from Bermuda so, with my natural tendency towards pre-trip anxiety, I just had to hold myself together and keep up the self-reassurance that I was actually feeling pretty healthy.

* * *

Christmas and the turn of the year passed without incident, involving just the customary mix of family fun and games, excessive eating and just a little more alcohol consumption than during the rest of the year. My pre-colonoscopy appointment was informative and reassuring and my general health still remained good. Although the concern would always be there in the back of my mind, I was determined to just keep it there and enjoy the experiences that Bermuda was waiting to offer.

With just a day to go, and with my suitcase packed, another unexpected bolt from the blue arrived. I received a text message from my dear friend and travel companion Clare to say that she would be unable to make the trip. Bill had been taken ill and was at the local hospital for tests on a possible heart condition. I felt so sorry for her, but clearly there was no other choice. Clare is naturally a very independent and resourceful person, not accustomed to showing her feelings when things don't go to plan, but when she stood on my doorstep a short time later to pass on some gifts that she had bought for our American friends, tears rolled down her cheeks. We shared a big hug and I vowed to bring back anything from the race series that she would have been entitled to.

While Clare's late withdrawal would clearly make no difference to my making the trip, it did rather unsettle the inner anxieties I was trying so hard to subdue. I had been finding that long-distance air travel with a companion was always so much less stressful, particularly as I grew older. I had also made perhaps not the cleverest of arrangements with regard to the journey itself. 2019 had been an expensive year, with the running trips to Easter Island, the Azores, Venice and Cyprus, and I had been quite keen to minimise my travel costs. There were direct flights from the UK to Bermuda, but a cheaper option was to fly to JFK airport in New York and then to travel to Bermuda from there. The downside was that this was a much longer journey, with several hours to pass at JFK, although this time would have gone much more quickly if I had had Clare's companionship. Now I faced a solo door-to-door journey of 24 hours of being awake, and trying to keep my cool.

But it went well. The highlight of the daytime transatlantic flight was perhaps the rudest airline steward I have ever come across, who seemed to have it in for every single passenger in his section of the plane. I also managed to keep my travel composure relatively calm, apart from one masterly moment of forgetfulness after arriving in New York, when I left both my passport and boarding card behind me at a security check after being hurried along through it. Fortunately I hadn't got far towards my next gate before I realised, and we were soon reunited.

It was with quite some relief that I eventually hauled my suitcase into our hotel in Hamilton, the capital of Bermuda. I explained to the lady at the check-in desk that I no longer had a room companion and was pleasantly surprised to be upgraded to a king-size single suite that had about as much floor space as my house at home!

It was late, very late, but I had noticed on the way in that the bar was still open. I made my way down and ordered a small glass of red wine; a personal reward for surviving the solo journey unscathed. The waiter brought it to my table and gave me the bill. TWENTY-ONE US DOLLARS! For one small glass of wine! Bermuda was not going to be a cheap trip. I savoured it slowly, declined the offer of a second glass, and then tip-toed off for a much-needed sleep.

* * *

With my American friends not due to arrive until the afternoon, I granted myself a good lie-in the next morning before going down for a leisurely breakfast. Despite the fatigue, I had had a fitful night's sleep and had been regularly woken by stormy winds and rain driving into the windows. When I did get up, however, the sun was shining and my first daylight view of Bermuda, out of the hotel window, was exactly how I imagined it: blue skies, a collection of small islands and tiny boats bobbing about on the water.

At breakfast, it was great to see a familiar face: Thom Gilligan, the founder and chief executive of Marathon Tours, and his partner, Joan. Thom had been a shipmate on the trip to Antarctica aboard the *Ioffe*, and we had got to know each other a little then. More relevant on this occasion was that Thom had a long track record of organising running events, at all levels, in Bermuda. Although he had taken a back seat for the past few years, the concept of a trio of challenging events had come from Thom originally, and new organisers had now invited him back to co-lead the festival, under the title of the Bermuda Triangle Challenge, named, of course, after the infamous area of the North Atlantic that had seen numerous boats and planes disappear.

Reading a copy of the *Royal Gazette* over my breakfast, the sheer scale and depth of the festival was quite something. It was based around a one-mile run, a 10km and either a full or half-marathon. For the one-mile race alone there were categories for primary school children, middle school children, senior school children and local adults, as well as male and female elite races, which included athletes of Olympian standard. You could pick and mix from the three distances, or you could go for the half or full marathon Bermuda Triangle Challenge. There was something for everyone and a chance for the tiniest child to tread the same route as medal-winning Olympians.

* * *

My first simple task was to source a supply of bottled water to make sure I stayed hydrated throughout the three days of racing, but my addled brain had clearly not learned the red wine lesson from the previous evening for, when I chose to buy two large bottles from the hotel shop, I was once again left staring in disbelief at the sales chit. However, a walk down to the town soon led to a garage that stocked water at a much more agreeable price, and gave me the chance to familiarise myself with, and take plenty of photographs of, the famous Front Street, lined on the land side with bars and restaurants. It would be the location of our first event.

Maybe this was a case of my ageing brain not thinking things through properly, but when I first booked this trip I visualised myself speeding along this seafront road in warm sunshine with vociferous, swimwear-clad crowds cheering us along. Bermuda is in the northern hemisphere however, it was January and the sun would have slid below the horizon long before the scheduled 6pm start. My pre-race visualisation definitely needed some re-editing.

* * *

Drew, Lynn and Liz all arrived at the hotel later that afternoon, and it was great to be back together again. Long-distance running friendships are a strange beast. You link up with someone from a totally different part of our world and maybe only spend a week or two in their company. Maybe it's the shared experience of the challenge that you face together, but those friendships tend to become very enduring, and if a future opportunity crops up to meet again you grasp it wholeheartedly.

Sadly for Liz the dream of the triangle challenge was already over. Her lower left leg was encased in a protective boot following an injury. However, boot or not, Liz was determined to walk the 10km route and go home with a medal, and she vowed to support us on the other two races. Lynn, a warm and friendly lady with a great sense of humour and, of course, of my own generation, had also set her sights on a walk/run of the 10km course. Drew was going for the triangle challenge but, unlike on Easter Island where he ran the full marathon, he had opted for the half this time with races on successive days.

That evening, we all attended the official opening ceremony of the running festival which was held just across the road from our hotel in the international headquarters of Bacardi rum; who knew their nerve centre was in such an exotic location? We stood in a magnificent large hall, one side entirely covered with a huge mural of exotic palm trees and a distant mountains setting, while overhead the deep blue ceiling was punctuated by a projected planetarium of the night sky. As we listened to a succession of speeches from local dignitaries outlining the history of the event, Liz quietly asked me if I recognised a young lady standing a few yards away. I did not, so Liz stepped across to speak to her. Within minutes our little party had increased by one.

Peg was yet another veteran of Antarctica 2018. She had travelled on the *Vavilov*, which was why Liz had recognised her and I hadn't, and, on this occasion, she was travelling alone so was pleased to link up with us. Like Drew and myself, Peg had signed up for the three-race, half-marathon triangle challenge. Together we all tucked in to the buffet food that was on offer, while out front, some of the elite athletes were being introduced to us, including Team GB's very own London and Rio Olympian, Eilish McColgan, who would be running the one-mile and the 10km races.

Another pleasing feature of the evening was the opportunity to try some of Bermuda's traditional rum cocktails. I have already whinged to you about the cost of that small glass of red wine on my first evening in Hamilton, and even the cost of water, but in Bermuda, and as would become apparent over the coming days, they either charge you the earth for a drink or they give it away. Complimentary Rum Swizzles and Dark 'n' Stormys washed the pasta down really well and brought a pleasing end to the first day of our running reunion.

* * *

Race day one dawned although no running was on the cards until the sun had gone down. For the second night in a row my sleep had been interrupted by the sound of howling winds and heavy rain being driven into the window panes. This was not the Bermuda I expected. After a light breakfast, and meeting up with Scott, our tour guide, the plan was that our little party would spend the morning together exploring more of Front Street. Although I was doing everything in my power to put the thought of my upcoming endoscopy to the back of my mind, a little bit of post-breakfast tummy disruption warranted a dip into my medication box for some Imodium, and I decided to play safe and explore the extensive hotel grounds and pools instead, although once again I was driven inside by rain. I had made my friends aware of my upcoming appointment; I didn't want them to think I was being unsociable.

When they returned in late morning, we visited the race expo together to pick up our race numbers and pack, which included a splendid and high-quality padded jacket with the race motif on the breast pocket. Happily, I was able to pick up the packet for Clare as well, so at least she would have something to show for the disappointment of missing the trip at the last minute. The expo was also the chance to see the rather unique medal arrangement that we had been given advance notice of. For obvious reasons, each medal was triangular-shaped, with a ribbon carrying the name of the race or series sponsor. Now, you will have to use your imagination here! For the one-mile, 10km and half-marathon, the medals were equilateral triangles pointing upwards. If you completed the whole series you were awarded a fourth medal which was an identically sized triangle, but pointing downwards. And here's the crunch. The individual medals had been magnetised so that when you arranged your three race medals together, there was a gap in the middle into which your series medal fitted, creating one large triangular Bermudan memento. All I had to do was to finish the races.

Still feeling a little less nauseous, I joined Liz, Drew, Lynn and Peg for a light pasta lunch down on Front Street and a very brief exploration of some of the shops.

Then it was back to the hotel to prepare for the evening mile event. In my pre-race planning, I had visualised myself striding down to Front Street in my vest and shorts, before exploding on to the one-mile flat route, a distance I probably hadn't run as a race since my school days, many decades ago. The reality was rather different. The howling wind was a constant. The heavy rain showers were more intermittent, and it felt cold. I hadn't come to Bermuda to be cold! A long-sleeved top now sat beneath my race vest. The calf supports, which I was using more often to prevent the cramps that I was increasingly suffering from as I grew older, at least kept my legs warmer. A waterproof hoodie would keep the rain off until I was ready to run, and with Liz and Lynn spectating on this race, I could leave it on until the last possible moment.

We gathered on a huge, hard-surfaced area, covered with a tarpaulin roof, at the edge of Hamilton harbour. The wind constantly threatened to rip the roof away but sturdy steel cables attached to giant blocks of concrete just about kept it in position. The school races had been taking place throughout the afternoon, but now it was our turn to take to the course. Because of the numbers involved we would be starting in waves as we were all chip-timed. Peg had been allocated wave four, while Drew and I would be in wave five. At the appropriate time we were led out into the starting pen and with the given signal, we were set on our way.

I'd like to say that I had rehearsed my pacing strategy for a mile race, but of course I hadn't. It was just a question of setting off a bit faster than a parkrun and then just trying to hang on. We initially headed west, into the wind, past a police traffic control pedestal lit with red lightbulbs, and then made a sharp 180-degree turn to run the length of Front Street, this time with wind pushing us from behind. Despite the adverse weather, the crowds lining the route were plentiful and vociferous and, for our wave at least, the rain temporarily held off.

At the end of Hamilton Docks, with just over a third of a mile to go, we turned again, this time feeling the full force of the headwind in our faces. I picked out people in front to try and overtake but my legs and lungs just weren't having it. And then, in what seemed no time at all, the finish line was there. About eight and a half minutes: I'd hoped for sub-eight but it wasn't to be. A very different running experience, nevertheless. My official finish line photo was very blurred, and I was happy to put that down to my extreme pace rather than the photographer using an inappropriate shutter speed. Race one was done and the first medal was hung around my neck.

With rain falling once again, we waited to catch a glimpse of the elite male and female races as they flashed by our sheltered viewpoint. How on earth can people run that fast for a mile? Subsequently we learned that Eilish McColgan had won the elite female race, although she wasn't twice as quick as me, and even the winning time in the male race, in the wind and rainswept conditions, was well outside the course record and around 15 seconds over the four-minute barrier. Perhaps that was why I failed to go sub-eight after all!

* * *

With a 9am start to the 10km race the following day it was a relatively early alarm, a quick croissant and coffee breakfast, and then a shuttle bus out to Bermuda's National Sports Centre where the race would start and finish. Overnight, the wind had moderated considerably and the rain clouds had drifted away, although it was still pretty chilly and I kept my outer layers on until the last possible moment before we were summoned to the start. We were all taking part in this one. Liz planned to walk the whole route, despite the heavy boot encasing her lower leg, and Drew would take on the course, alongside Lynn.

As we were walked out on to the lane outside the centre to the start area, the very first thing I noticed was a rather steep hill, and yes, that was the way we were running. We wished each other good luck and I settled down towards the rear of the field, the walkers being set off five minutes after the runners. With the conditions being a lot more conducive to running, the initial climb was soon conquered and I quickly settled into a good rhythm as we swung eastwards and downhill on a traffic-free road, running through the centre of the main island, unimaginatively named Middle Road. At two miles the route climbed again, steeply and for much longer, but every hill has a top to it, and the inevitable downhill soon followed.

Now we were heading for the Flatts Village district; in days gone by, a small inlet here would provide access for small boats eager to avoid the eagle eyes of the customs officials present at the island's main port. We swung left and left again, and followed the main road running along the north coast of the island, and yes, it was called North Shore Road. This section was relatively flat, and all felt good as I took in the stunning views out to sea, but as I approached eight kilometres and the road started to swing back inland, another steep hill came into view, and it was as if my brain switched off my fuel supply. I guess it is all part of life's journey, but it irks me to have to slow to a walk on a race as short as 10km. In the past it wouldn't have happened, but this was the present and, hopefully, there will still be plenty of future ahead.

The voice of reason inside my skull reminded me that it was definitely getting warmer, and that I still had a hilly half-marathon ahead of me the following morning. Bermuda just doesn't do flat but this hill, too, had a summit and from there I ran every step, even sprinting to the finish line on the track in the sports centre. Job done and medal number two was hung around my neck, but there was just a tinge of disappointment that I hadn't been able to run every step.

* * *

Peg finished just seconds behind me although we hadn't encountered each other during the run itself, and we waited together trackside for our friends to finish.

Sometime later, Liz strode over the line in her medical boot, followed shortly afterwards by Drew finishing alongside Lynn. We all now had medals to show for our efforts.

I know I have been guilty of grumbling about the cost of everything in Bermuda, but I was about to take all that back. Our race information pack had promised refreshments after we left the finish chute, and I was expecting the usual bottle of water and perhaps a banana. What we entered, however, was a finish area that would rival any race on the planet. Yes, there was water, but also a wide choice of soft drinks, fruit juices, local beer on tap and, of course, the traditional Dark 'n' Stormy rum cocktails. There were bananas, but also many other varieties of fruit, snacks, sandwiches and energy bars and, to cap it all, everything was free! It could have been a recipe for disaster with a half-marathon to complete the following day but I managed to keep myself in check, just about, although that doesn't mean I didn't partake of the beer and cocktails on offer.

There was a real party atmosphere in the finish area, and we were royally entertained by a local group of Gombey dancers, an iconic symbol of Bermuda's African, Caribbean and British heritage. An infectious and relentless mixture of dance, masquerade and drumming, the Gombeys of all ages skipped, swerved and twirled among us in their long-legged costumes of every colour imaginable, their faces hidden behind vibrant masks, and their towering hats crowned with clusters of long bird feathers.

The festive proceedings were brought to a close with the presentation of the 10km race awards and, again, there was further cause for celebration with Thom Gilligan picking up the runners-up trophy in his age category and our own marvellous super-mum, Lynn, picking up the third place trophy in her age group.

* * *

With the running and celebrating completed by midday, it was a slightly inebriated group of friends that spent the afternoon exploring what else Bermuda had to offer, in a trip around the main island in a hired taxi. The Royal Naval Dockyard, which served as a major western Atlantic base for the British Royal Navy until the 1950s, was now a tourist attraction, hosting massive cruise liners during the summer months and acting as a gateway to the island's other charms. On the way there we visited many picturesque, remote beaches and coves, including the famous Glass Beach, and, for the first time since our arrival, the sun was now really beginning to make its presence felt; not particularly timely with the following day's half-marathon in mind.

Our final stop was to visit the cast-iron Gibb's Hill lighthouse tower, perched on top of one of Bermuda's tallest hills and constructed by the Royal Engineers back in 1844; apparently its light can be seen by aircraft 100 miles away, and there were certainly magnificent views of Bermuda's many islands from up there.

The eve of the long stage, whether we were running full or half-marathon, was marked by the official pasta dinner, accompanied by a few speeches and an on-stage interview, quite harrowing at times, with the American Olympian middle-distance runner Suzy Favor Hamilton, describing her journey through track glory, bipolar disorder and prostitution. Sipping iced water only after my slight cocktail excesses of the late morning, I didn't find it a comfortable listen that might calm my pre-race jitters, but nevertheless I recognised the courage it must have taken to be so brutally honest in order to raise awareness for others on a similar journey.

* * *

It was not the most confident version of me that lined up on the start line for the half-marathon the following morning. Whether that was due to a bit of anxiety that I had resorted to some walking on the previous day's 10km stage, or just the residual nervousness about my upcoming investigations, it was one of those days when a half-marathon seemed an awfully long way.

At least we didn't have far to travel, or fuss around with depositing baggage, as the start area was immediately outside the front of our hotel. With Liz and Lynn once again spectating, I took my place towards the rear of the field alongside Drew and Peg. The weather was still set fair, the breeze was much lighter and the temperature was edging upwards towards a slightly more uncomfortable level. At the sound of a klaxon we set off gently downhill, soon passing the Barr's Bay Park area, which would mark the finish, and then through the city of Hamilton where Liz and Lynn shouted encouragement from the sidelines. I soon settled into a steady, chatty pace alongside Peg and after a couple of miles we turned south towards the Camden district where we joined the southern coastal road with magnificent views out to sea.

Despite my earlier misgivings, I was feeling OK until shortly after the four-mile marker when we encountered a steep hill. After chastising myself for not managing to run up a similar gradient the day before, I was determined to conquer this one and, with arms pumping and head held high, I drove myself up what seemed like an endless slope. Success! I paused briefly at the top and looked back for Peg but there was no sign of her among the many who had resorted to walking so I pushed on, giving myself a virtual pat on the back for conquering a personal challenge. In retrospect, the climb had taken a lot more out of me than I had suspected at the time and, from six miles onwards, I did resort to using a run-walk strategy to keep the momentum going forward. Count 50 or 100 paces of walking, or identify a lamp-post ahead where you will start running again, but keeping on the move at all costs.

The Bermudan spectators were awesome. Standing outside their often opulent properties, they cheered, clapped and coaxed us along the gently undulating route as we reached the North Shore Road, part of which we had run the previous day. An all-female percussion group, clad in blue, beat out an infectious rhythm on their colourful drums that seemed perfectly timed to coincide with the tempo of our feet. We clapped as we ran and it was a truly joyous interaction between those that ran and those that didn't.

Although the temperature was now beginning to climb even further, there were water stations almost every mile and, uniquely for this race, there were also two aid stations where Bermudan rum was served! You will know by now that I had developed a taste for this local liquor, but even I had to pass on this treat during a half-marathon. Keeping the walk breaks as short as possible, my overall pace was still pretty good and, more importantly, was not getting slower and slower. I began to visualise the finish line, receiving my third medal and then the final challenge medal, to complete the large magnetic triangle. But there was to be one more major test to face; I was suddenly confronted with what we runners call a Paula Radcliffe moment.

In all my decades of running many thousands of miles, across deserts and icecaps, and up and down mountain trails, I have never reached a point during a race, where I just HAD to find a toilet, and we are not talking about a wee in the bush here. Perhaps the nearest experience had been in the Rio de Janeiro half-marathon in 2016 when I, among many others, had been struck down by a vicious tummy bug just two days before the race. Thanks to the powers of copious amounts of Imodium I had made it to the start line and only began to suffer in the very final half a mile, developing powerful gluteus maximus contractions to get me over the line, and to quickly find the toilet facilities in the finish area. In Bermuda, I still had over three miles to run and there was no way on earth I could manage that.

We were passing through a very salubrious residential area. Did I really have the courage to ask some of the people standing outside their posh homes if I could use their loo? I was getting to the point where even any sort of movement was risky when ahead I saw a sight that I will forever be so grateful for: a yellow portaloo. It was vacant. I shudder to think of the consequences had it been occupied.

Two minutes later I was back on the road again and feeling mightily relieved in more ways than one. I still had almost three miles to go, I was still having to resort to a few paces of walking on some of the uphill sections, but I was now in that happy place where I knew it would take a freak event to stop me from crossing the finish line. Just occasionally, one of the full marathon runners would come past me and I would urge them on. They had started from the Royal Dockyards some two hours before us, so these guys were heading for a time of just over four hours. As we swung eastwards next to Hamilton harbour, I caught sight of Liz standing by the roadside, camera in hand. I asked her if Peg had come through but she hadn't; I thought perhaps that she had overtaken me while I was otherwise engaged in my cabin of relief. I ran past our hotel where the start had taken place and then there was just another half a mile to go before I passed under the green and pink inflatable finish arch: the Bermuda Triangle Challenge was complete.

It was an OK time; some ten minutes slower than my road half-marathon on Easter Island just over six months previously, but a good deal quicker than my two most recent trail half-marathons in the Azores and Cyprus. Given my general health concerns, and the enforced pit stop en route, I was happy to take that and headed straight for the water bottles to replace the fluid I had lost.

Peg finished just a couple of minutes behind me and was delighted to announce that she had taken advantage of the rum stops on the way; the carefree exuberance of youth. With medals hung around our necks we then made full use of the once-again generous offerings at the finish festival, firstly with some thirst-quenching beer and then, once Drew had crossed the line, several excursions to the Dark 'n' Stormy queue. The running was done, the challenge was completed, and we could really let our hair down to celebrate.

It was during this time of laughter, tipsiness and frivolity that I heard my name called out over the public address system as having finished third in my age group for the half-marathon challenge. Just as in Cyprus two months previously, advancing years, and still being able to run at a reasonable pace, was producing rewards. Still clutching my rum cocktail in one hand, I stepped forward to collect my trophy from a Bermudan government minister to loud applause from the Marathon Tours contingent.

It was a fitting end to a testing trip: from the lows of Clare's late withdrawal and my own health concerns, to the highs of running on such a beautiful island in the company of fabulous friends, old and new. All that was left to endure was those wasted hours sitting at JFK on the way back and, once again, regretting the decision not to fly directly for the sake of a few quid.

* * *

Just over a week after I set foot back on British soil, I underwent the colonoscopy. By far the most brutal part of it was the 'cleansing' process the day before, and not being the bravest of souls, I opted to have the procedure itself carried out under sedation. It was quite a surreal experience to lie there on your side and view the internal surfaces of your lower intestine, as if you were watching a movie on the television. The doctor identified a large polyp growing on the inner wall, skilfully lassoed it with a wire noose and removed it for further examination. Other than that, he seemed fairly optimistic about what he had seen and, after a nervy five-day wait, the polyp was identified as non-malignant, although it would have had the potential to turn nasty if it had remained where it was. I breathed a huge sigh of relief. For the second time in a few years, after the lung incident in 2015, the C-word had raised its head but had proved to be a false alarm, at least for now. A reminder that no great running journeys last forever.

For now though, I had the all-clear, and the prospect of preparing myself for overseas half-marathons on the streets of Prague and volcanic craters of Iceland. But life was about to take an unexpected twist; not just for me, but for everybody on the planet.

Chapter 9

It's a crazy world out there

IF YOU have been following my story from the very beginning, you will know that this is the third book of describing my running adventures all around the world – and in all sorts of climatic conditions. And yet, as I sit here now at my keyboard, I know that this will probably be the hardest chapter of all to write. Not so much about running as about not running, or at least running under very restrictive conditions. Where do you begin?

Let's start with some positivity. After a successful trip to Bermuda, and the enormous sigh of relief following my medical investigations, I began my annual home campaign with my traditional first race of the year, a 12km road course near to Stratford-upon-Avon at the end of January. A challenging route but the weather was kind and I finished comfortably, although my time confirmed the not unexpected gradual slowing as the years ticked by.

But rumbling in the background was a news story that started in China where a new respiratory virus was causing panic and leading to new hospitals being erected in a matter of days to accommodate the increasing number of sufferers. Within weeks the focus of the news channels had moved to regions in the north of Italy, particularly Lombardy and Veneto, areas where I had been running just a few months previously. Hospitals and intensive care units were overflowing with critically ill patients and a crisis that none of us could have envisaged just a few months earlier was unfolding and would reach every corner of our world. Inevitably, Covid-19 arrived on the shores of the UK; in fact the second case to be confirmed was at the very hospital where I had begun my working life, in Brighton.

The crisis deepened. Manufacturing companies were asked to turn their attention to building ventilators, exhibition centres and other large venues were being transformed into emergency Nightingale hospitals and a frantic search was on to source more and more personal protective equipment for health and care staff, much of it turning out to be pretty useless, but that's another story that belongs in somebody else's book.

In mid-March I drove down to Sussex for a weekend to celebrate my daughter Angela's birthday, which would be followed a few days later by granddaughter Josie's birthday. Little did I know that this would be the last time I would see them in person for well over a year. On the Saturday morning I completed my 349th parkrun in Eastbourne with Angela on a rather wet and rainy day. With the government openly discussing the banning of large gatherings, I did wonder how long it might be before I ran my 350th.

The following morning, in somewhat more pleasant weather conditions, I had the great pleasure of running alongside Josie on only her second junior parkrun on an out-and-back course along Eastbourne promenade. After vigorously joining in with the warm-up exercises she sprinted away from me on the 'go' signal, but soon settled back into a much more sensible pace for her. By the turn-around point at halfway, interest was beginning to wane a little, so we invented a few mind games to keep the forward momentum going. We swam across imaginary rivers, swerved around crocodiles and sprinted away from chasing tigers. Before too long we turned a bend and there were her mum and dad waiting to cheer her across the finishing line. I may have been lucky enough to run in some amazing places around the planet, but little moments like these make my running journey so joyous.

Even as we walked back to Angela's car afterwards, my vibrating phone revealed a breaking news story that the government were considering requiring everyone over 70 years old to remain indoors: the storm clouds were gathering. Just a few days later, parkruns across the UK were suspended, and on 23 March a solemn prime minister appeared on our television screens to tell us that we must all stay at home. Lockdown one had begun.

* * *

I have no intention of giving a blow-by-blow account of my experiences throughout the pandemic lockdowns.

Every single person reading this has their own stories to tell, many of them distressing and, in some cases, tragic. I didn't have to worry about losing my job and my income, I didn't have elderly relatives to care for and worry about, and I didn't have young children to home school. My only real burden was keeping myself occupied without the social support I would normally get from family, my running groups, parkrun, University of the Third Age meetings and, of course, giving my running talks.

To begin with I was determined to make use of the one period a day we were permitted outdoors for local exercise, albeit alone. I planned out a 6km circular route, starting and finishing at home, and one that I knew would be very quiet so that socially distancing two metres from others would not be a problem. As it was a circle, I could change direction on alternate days, and I slightly tweaked the 'run alone' rule by taking my neighbour's dog Betsy with me to give her some welcome exercise.

All went well for a couple of weeks, although occasionally Betsy would back away from me when I went to collect her, so I introduced a few more rest days into her exercise programme. For some weeks I had been experiencing slight pain in my left foot around the metatarsal area. It didn't seem to be getting any worse, but neither was it improving. And then, after a strenuous day of digging in the back garden, my run the following morning was rapidly cut short by right knee pain. For a week I iced it, elevated it and rubbed painkilling gels into it, before jogging slowly around routes of barely two kilometres, but it wasn't to be. Complete rest was the only answer. Throughout my running life I have been so lucky with injuries, so a self-enforced lay-off of three weeks seemed like forever. It was hard mentally as well. Although socialising with others was still very much off the cards, at least if you were out for a run you could say hello to people you passed, and that really seemed to help the growing feeling of isolation and loneliness.

Initial signs were encouraging when I again began some short runs on soft surfaces; I even managed a 5km run without too much discomfort, but two days later another run ended less than 100 yards from my front door with a sudden and sharp pain below my right kneecap. The time for self-help was over; I needed professional advice. Getting face-to-face appointments with a physio was out of the question, but I managed to access an online physiotherapist over Zoom who diagnosed relatively minor problems with the medial ligament and patellar tendon, and gave me a series of strengthening exercises to do twice a day, with strict instructions not to resume running until given the go-ahead at follow-up appointments. Well, if there was a good time to have an injury, then this was it as I wouldn't be missing out on any races, home or abroad.

So where did the land lie with regard to upcoming overseas adventures, and what impact would the pandemic have? You may remember that I had previously entered the Iceland Volcano half-marathon, due to be run in the summer of 2020, but this was the first of my races to fall victim to the virus. Having missed out on our Bermuda trip at the very last minute, my travelling companion Clare had also entered this race, but now we would both have to wait for a further 12 months.

In a moment of sheer optimism, possibly influenced again by a glass or two of red wine, I had also entered another half-marathon in Madagascar, due to take place in June 2020. This was while recuperating from my knee problems; perhaps I just needed another light at the end of the tunnel, and once again Clare was up for the challenge. This also fell victim to the pandemic.

And then there was the Prague half-marathon, and our much anticipated reunion with our American friends from the Easter Island trip. This race had taken on extra significance for me back in October 2019 when the Superhalfs series had been announced. With Prague and Cardiff already signed up for in 2020, it would have left me two years to complete the runs in Copenhagen, Lisbon and Valencia, and I had even got as far as putting some provisional dates in my diary for those.

If ever a major new race series was launched at the wrong time, however, then it has to have been the Superhalfs. The springtime Prague race was its first casualty of Covid, and was initially postponed to a date in the autumn of 2020 – the very same day as the proposed Cardiff race. I would have to have been a Time Lord to have achieved that! Subsequently, a whole string of postponements followed in each of the host cities and it wouldn't be until 2022 that the series would finally be able to get off the ground. You have to have some sympathy for those behind the project.

* * *

At this point, I'd like to take a little break from talking about my own experiences to pay tribute to two very special ladies who each, in very different ways, played an important role in my running life. Both lost their lives in 2020, at far too young an age, to cancer.

The first is Helen, my next-door neighbour. One of the hardest aspects of my travelling adventures was knowing that I would be leaving my feline house companion, Nougat, on her own for long periods, and that she would miss me dreadfully. Nougat had made it clear at an early age that she would not tolerate a cattery by going on hunger strike, so leaving her in her familiar surroundings at home was always the best option, with helpful neighbours coming in to feed her twice a day. My southern hemisphere trips to Australia, New Zealand and Antarctica meant that I was away for several weeks at a time, so Helen not only fed Nougat but found the time to give her the companionship that she was missing. I had approached Helen to see if she could again help out while I was in Bermuda but she said it was probably best to find someone else as she was having hospital tests for abdominal pain. On my return, I discovered that Helen had been diagnosed with stage four pancreatic cancer and, despite a typically brave fight, she succumbed to this cruel illness in July of 2020. Not just a neighbour, but a caring and supportive friend lost.

My second awesome and hugely missed lady was Lizzie Tovey. The very first time I met Lizzie, she was running around our local lake with a good friend of mine, Corin. Lizzie was at the very beginning of what turned out to be a tragically short but spectacular running journey. In her 30s, Lizzie, an outgoing and bubbly personality, began to lose her sight. Eventually she was to lose almost all of the sight in her right eye, and only retained a small amount of central vision in her other eye. Feeling depressed and lacking confidence, Lizzie sought ways that could get her out into the fresh air. Through a charity she made contact with Corin, who had just registered as a guide runner for the visually impaired, and together they embarked on a couch to 5k programme, culminating in Lizzie's first parkrun, at our local Arrow Valley lake, in April 2018.

Lizzie loved the atmosphere and sense of inclusion of parkrun and not only as a runner, as she also loved to volunteer. Our parkrun route at the time was two laps of the lake, which included a fairly demanding hill climb on each circuit, affectionately known to the participants as 'Cardiac Hill'. Lizzie, with her husband Mark, would regularly stand at the top of this hill, where the runners took a sharp left turn, and bellow encouragement to the runners as they struggled up the incline.

Soon, other members of Lizzie's growing circle of running friends took on the task of taking hold of the other end of her tether and guiding her; it became a badge of honour to run with Lizzie. With ever-growing confidence she began to run longer distance, and incredibly, just 12 months after her very first parkrun, and with Corin as her guide, Lizzie completed the 2019 London Marathon. However, that was only part of the story of that race. Lizzie was furious, to put it mildly, when she discovered before the race that Corin would not receive a finishers' medal, or even appear in the official results, for guiding her around the 26.2-mile course. She began a vigorous media campaign to get all guide runners the recognition that they deserved and, in the end, the organising committee of the London Marathon relented, and changed the ruling. Another Lizzie victory.

A further epic Lizzie achievement came in December of 2019 when she completed her beloved Arrow Valley parkrun without being tethered to anybody. Surrounded by a Kipchoge-style posse of her running friends to keep her safe and to shout instructions, she ran freely for the entire 5km course and the emotion of the moment as she crossed the finish line came out in a flood of tears.

But if sight loss at such an early age wasn't enough for Lizzie to have to cope with, life was about to deliver another devastating blow to her. For some time on her running outings with friends, Lizzie would suffer episodes of motion sickness which would sometimes lead to her run being cut short. Lizzie had attributed these symptoms of vertigo to her sight problems. Sadly, it was far more serious than that. Just a few weeks before we had gone into the first lockdown, Lizzie revealed that scans had shown that the motion sickness was being caused by tumours pressing on her neck and around her throat, and in February 2020, she was diagnosed with an aggressive and, sadly, terminal breast cancer.

With her limitless supply of raw courage and positivity, Lizzie embarked on a series of challenging chemotherapy cycles. These would leave her immunocompromised and with Covid beginning to spread rapidly, Lizzie was confined to indoors. But did this put an end to her new-found love of running? Not a bit of it! Dressing up in her trademark colourful leggings, and sometimes even in fancy dress, Lizzie would run on 'Terry the Treadmill' indoors, while linking remotely with her many running friends outdoors.

When the first lockdown passed, Lizzie even took on the 2020 virtual London Marathon, breaking down the total distance into shorter, manageable segments, with a few socially distanced friends to support her. Despite enduring some bad reactions from her treatment, Lizzie managed to complete the full distance within the allotted 24 hours at Arrow Valley lake, raising huge amounts of money for her favourite charities.

I never had the honour of actually running with Lizzie. We would often chat at parkruns and she came along to listen to several of my talks. Lizzie also loved my two previous books, writing glowing reviews of them online and advocating how much they helped her deal with her own mental tussles when the going got tough. The final time I spoke to Lizzie, I was out on a solo run around a six-mile route I had discovered during the first lockdown. As I alluded to in an earlier chapter of this book, we runners sometimes get obsessed with Strava art; drawing recognisable objects as the overhead satellites track our progress around a route. This particular run drew a Tyrannosaurus Rex-type outline, and became known on Strava as 'Doug's Dinosaur'.

As I ran along the route, a familiar voice called out to me from the opposite side of the road. It was my friend Sonia, a local running legend in her own right (who else would choose to run 50 miles around our lake on the day she celebrated her 50th birthday!), and she was out for a walk with Lizzie. Sonia was Lizzie's Macmillan support buddy, and had been by her side almost constantly since the very first days of her diagnosis. We stopped and chatted for a few minutes, and Lizzie said that when she felt a bit stronger she would love to join me for a walk around 'Doug's Dinosaur'. Sadly, it was not to be; Lizzie passed away on Boxing Day of 2020.

Aside from the devastation felt by Mark and her close family, Lizzie had made such an impact on so many people in her all too short life. Her indomitable spirit, in the greatest of adversity, had earned her a place in the hearts of so many in the local running community. Sonia arranged a collection that paid for a memorial bench that was placed on the very corner at the top of the hill of the parkrun route where Lizzie and Mark used to bellow their encouragement, and even managed to persuade our local council to officially name the location 'Tovey Corner'.

I am honoured to dedicate this book to the memory of Lizzie Tovey: courage beyond words.

* * *

So let's return to the gloomy days of lockdowns and the attempts to restore at least some sort of normality to my running routine. To be absolutely frank and honest, Covid tested me in ways that I would never have imagined. Once my online physiotherapist had given me the go-ahead to resume some gentle, soft-surface running I was back out there, but the weeks and months of isolation had taken a toll on my usually strong mental resolve. There had, of course, been some light-hearted moments during the lockdown to break up the monotony. I enjoyed an impromptu 72nd birthday celebration with a few thirsty neighbours as we sat spaced well apart on our front drives enjoying a beer in the May sunshine. As groceries were delivered to our doorsteps by supermarket vans, there was amusement when my house welcomed a delivery van from the local brewery, and for several months I enjoyed the luxury of 'click and collect' Sunday roast dinners from a nearby hostelry. Even collecting my cat's prescription drugs from the otherwise-deserted rear car park of a local pet store took on the appearance of a dodgy 'drug drop'.

Eventually we were allowed to run with another socially distanced friend and then the 'rule of six' came into operation. This had two great benefits as far as my social isolation was concerned. Firstly, our Crabbs Cross Chasers running group could begin meeting again. We had enough qualified run leaders to take charge of the smaller groups and we staggered start times and meeting places to ensure we kept within the guidelines. It was also around this time that I had discovered the 'Doug's

Dinosaur' route, and I had numerous requests from running friends who wanted to add it to their Strava profiles. Again, with five others, the journey became an increasingly regular part of my running programme.

There were some frustrating anomalies thrown up by the government's regulations too. I happen to live just a few hundred yards from a county border and, when the tier system was in place, we had the crazy situation of having friends from just over the border suddenly becoming *personae non gratae* when it came to running with us. But we made the most of what were challenging times as case rates fluctuated.

As 2020 drew to a close with yet another surge in infections, it became apparent that, for the first time in my life, I would spend Christmas Day alone, and this was where the running community was at its finest. With starter and dessert as well, a full turkey roast was delivered to my doorstep by kind-hearted running friends!

I continued to make steady progress as we moved through 2021, although my right knee would probably never be 100 per cent again and would always need some sort of support to keep it stable. Endurance was now my quandary, with anything beyond four or five miles leading to those little voices in my head urging me to take a break; my instinct was that it was a mental issue rather than physical.

And then on a sunny morning at the end of June 2021, my self-confidence took yet another blow. I was running with a small group of our Crabbs Cross Chasers on a trail route when, in an instant, my forehead suddenly made heavy impact with the ground. I wasn't knocked unconscious as I remember my friend Mick, whom I was running alongside, calling out to those further ahead to stop. As you will know by now, I had become increasingly prone to falls while out running in recent years, but the huge majority of these had been a matter of giving myself a couple of minutes to recompose, and then continuing on to home where I could treat the cuts and grazes on hands, elbows and knees. This time I knew there would be no continuing.

While friends cleaned up the blood from the inevitable grazes, I knew the significant impact had been my head. It seemed I had caught my toe on the remnants of an old wooden fence post that was protruding from the trail by just a centimetre or two. Already I could feel a large lump forming on my forehead and flashes of light were spinning as I looked up at the sky. About 500 metres away was a museum of Redditch's industrial past and one of my running friends, Pauline, went to see if they had some ice. She returned with Amanda, who was the museum's first-aider, who proceeded to bathe my forehead. I was cold and shivering violently and, as if by magic, both foil and woollen blankets arrived from the museum, and an ambulance was called as I wasn't going anywhere under my own steam very soon. It started to rain and, once again, a magical umbrella was produced from nowhere for Amanda to hold over my head. The wait for the ambulance seemed interminable and now a second swelling was growing out of my right forearm; I feared I might have broken a bone in the fall.

Eventually, two cheery paramedics arrived, assessed me and deemed it safe for me to be taken back along the trail in a wheelchair to the ambulance, which was parked at the museum. I was taken to our local accident and emergency department, placed into a neck brace, and underwent various tests and examinations for the next few hours. Thankfully the arm swelling was soft tissue damage and not a fracture, and eventually I was discharged, provided someone stayed with me overnight in case of delayed concussion. My son Chris was already on his way down from Telford and enjoyed the experience of drinking my wine that evening while my battered features sipped at the glass of water I was permitted.

I had been lucky, very lucky, but it was a watershed moment and some lessons had to be learned to try and stop it happening again. Falling during a run had been an increasingly annoying habit but this could have been so much worse. It was not until a couple of weeks later that I truly appreciated how much of the head impact had been taken by the peaked cap I was wearing at the time. Mick had taken it home to wash once I was on my way to the hospital. When he examined it closely he realised that would be futile. He messaged me to say it had probably saved me from a far more serious injury but it was not until I was finally reunited with my cap and saw the crumpled peak and ripped fabric for myself that I truly appreciated his words. From that day onwards

I would always wear a peaked cap, a visor or a front-padded woolly hat, just in case.

The other major change related to my glasses that I always wore during running. I wear varifocal lenses. Could the constant switching from looking at the ground to see where my feet were landing, and then looking into the distance ahead, cause me to miss a few bumps on the route? I tended to use an older pair of glasses for running to protect my best pair, and the ones I was wearing on this occasion were not only smashed beyond repair but also caused quite a bit of damage to my nose and eye sockets.

Could I run without wearing glasses at all? My distance vision was pretty clear anyway and my eyes were far enough above the ground to see where my feet were landing. Could the switching between different parts of the varifocal lens be a contributory factor? I experimented with a few parkruns without wearing glasses and all went well. There was only one downside. While my vision was adequate during daylight, there was no way I could see well enough in the dark without my glasses on. I had to make the difficult decision to stop night running, which was hard as one of my running groups runs in darkness during the winter months, but, as a retired person, I could always find time during the daylight hours to fit in my runs.

As a postscript to this story, and I really don't want to jinx anything, as I write this piece some 18 months after my big fall, the experiment of running without wearing glasses appears to be a success!

* * *

After a couple of false starts, life seemed to be slowly returning to some sort of normality when, at the end of July 2021, parkrun finally returned after a break of 71 weeks. At long last I would be able to bring up number 350. There was just a tinge of disappointment associated with it, though. Ongoing renewal works of the footpaths around our lovely Arrow Valley lake meant that we would have to find a new route and, sadly, it wouldn't be possible to include Tovey Corner in it. Nevertheless, our core team worked hard to find a new three-lap trail route in a different area of the park. Although running around the perimeter of some football pitches might not qualify as a trail run by some, there certainly were sections that revealed the natural beauty of the park and, at the end of each lap, there was a challenging steep ramp to overcome.

It's fair to say that trail running is not everybody's cup of tea, particularly those who are a bit less nimble on their feet (which I suppose should include me!), so attendances fell to about half or less of what they were prior to lockdown. Furthermore, as summer turned to autumn and the rains increased, sections of the route became something of a mudfest, and that final ramp became increasingly difficult to summit.

But good news was around the corner. By the beginning of 2022, the path works at the lake had been completed and, in February of that year, our parkrun returned to a revised and improved route that took in even more views of the lake. Most importantly we would again run past Tovey Corner, and at the inaugural run it was fitting that Lizzie's husband Mark was a marshal at that point, as we acknowledged her presence as we ran past her memorial bench.

* * *

Just a few days later I would hear further tragic news of just how cruel life can be. For those of my readers who read my previous book, *Can We Run With You, Grandfather?*, you may remember that there was another Doug on board our ship, *Ioffe*, on our adventure in Antarctica. I never really got to know Douglas Denys very well on the trip, other than to know that we both came from medical backgrounds – Doug was an ear, nose and throat surgeon – and we both had a successful Marathon des Sables finish on our running CVs. Shortly after the Antarctica trip, Doug showed us another of his many talents when he produced a detailed, hand-drawn map of the Antarctic Peninsula, illustrated with drawings of our ship, penguins, seals and whales, with many of the landmarks and bays named after the people he had shared the journey with, including a Doug Richards Point in the north of the Weddell Sea. In a typically generous gesture, Doug offered to send a high-resolution copy of his drawing to any of his ship-mates, so that we could get it printed in any form that we wanted. I have a three foot by two foot canvas hanging on my lounge wall, and it is a precious reminder of one of the greatest trips of my lifetime.

After the trip, the *Ioffe* runners had kept in touch with one another through social media and, in the early months of 2022, Doug had posted that he was about to undergo complex heart surgery, and asked for our prayers. Tragically, at the age of just 44, Doug did not survive the operation. It was only when I read an obituary just a few days later that I learned that he had been born with a congenital heart deformity, and had written about his life, struggles and achievements in his own book, *Rhythm of a Runner*. What an inspiring read. Our paths had only crossed for a precious few days, but I feel honoured to have met a man who achieved so much in such a short lifetime, and my wall canvas became an even more precious possession.

* * *

As signs of spring 2022 began to lift our spirits, the government decreed, perhaps rather prematurely, that it was time to 'live with Covid' and lifted all remaining restrictions in the UK. On that very same day, the Russian army invaded Ukraine, and the planet was plunged into a totally different kind of turmoil.

It's a crazy world out there.

Chapter 10

The tipping point

FOR THE very first time in over two years, an overseas running adventure was looking increasingly likely to actually happen. The Prague half-marathon had originally been planned as a European reunion with several of our American friends made on Easter Island. In the interim I had been reunited for a few days with Liz and Drew in Bermuda, the trip Clare sadly had to withdraw from at the very last minute, but the hopes of a larger gathering centred on Prague.

Originally scheduled for the end of March 2020, the race became one of the very first victims of the pandemic, with the date being moved back on several occasions only to be thwarted again by the march of the virus. Now, as restrictions were slowly and haphazardly being lifted in many parts of the world, the first weekend in April 2022 was looking as if it would finally get the green light. Our hotel had been very obliging in continually moving our booking dates, but now perhaps was the time to start looking at flights.

But how was I feeling about an imminent return to running and travel, something that I had become so used to over the years? The simple answer was with some unease. In the past I had often travelled alone to distant parts of the world, not meeting anyone associated with the forthcoming adventure until I reached the final destination. Now, a short trip into central Europe and in the company of Clare was giving rise to a few sleepless nights. There was definitely something different about my mindset post-Covid.

As ever with anxiety, it was hard to put a finger on whatever was triggering the problem. Everybody reacted differently to the pandemic. On a scale of one to ten, with the Covid-deniers at one and those heavily at risk of a bad outcome due to existing medical conditions or treatment at ten, I was right towards the top end of that scale. With my past history of tuberculosis and psittacosis my lungs were already heavily scarred, as had been discovered in my brush with pneumonia five years previously. I wasn't prepared to take any risk of further lung problems so avoided indoor meetings whenever possible and always wore a mask when close to others, whether inside or out.

Loneliness had definitely been an issue, with living alone and not having close family nearby. Of course I had the company of my ever-faithful cat, Nougat, and I would never underestimate how much that companionship kept me going through the darker days of lockdown. Someone to talk to, to share your problems with, but someone who clearly cared about me as well.

Whenever I had to get up to use the bathroom during the night, Nougat would suddenly appear at my feet and then lead me back to my side of my bed, her tail bolt upright, like the flag of a guide leading a tour party.

That changed in September 2021. I woke one morning to find Nougat in a collapsed state and seemingly unable to see, having suffered some sort of cerebral event. She rallied briefly for a couple of days, following some intravenous fluids, but then deteriorated rapidly again. I knew it was that time that every pet owner dreads and after 15 years of unconditional love from both parties, it was time to say goodbye.

The house then seemed really empty, and the feelings of social isolation grew even greater. I was not the only one in the close family to be suffering from pet bereavement either. Chris had lost his pet cat Tipsy a few months before Nougat's death, strangely in very similar circumstances, and then just 12 days after Nougat left us, Chris lost his wonderful German shepherd husky cross, Tizer, a dog I had shared so many happy memories with.

Should I get another cat? I had owned cats for as long as I could remember but my birthday count now seemed to be advancing faster than I would have liked, and it would be only fair to consider what the feline's longer-term outlook might be; they can live for 20 years or longer. After just a few weeks of having no other life in the house to talk to, I convinced myself that my health was good enough to take on the responsibility of pet ownership once more. I could have taken an older rescue cat but then didn't want the risk of losing another beloved pet in maybe a few years' time. In the end I set my heart on getting a young rescue cat, albeit not a tiny kitten, but then Chris threw another spanner into the works. His plan to replace Tipsy and Tizer was to get two kittens, so that they would have each other's company when he was out of the house. This set more thoughts rolling.

One of the hardest parts of my overseas running adventures had been leaving Nougat for sometimes weeks at a time. She had made it clear from an early age that boarding was not for her so always stayed at home, with free access to her cat flap and kind neighbours like the much-missed Helen coming in twice a day to feed her. If I went for the two young cats option, at least they would have each other's company if I were to return to my running travels. I made an appointment to visit a local cat rescue sanctuary.

Soft to the core, the first two cats I was shown melted my heart and I knew immediately that they were for me. They were sisters, one tabby and white, and the other black and white. Born feral on farmland, they had been taken on by a foster carer to socialise them and then kept until they were old enough to be chipped and neutered. Six to seven months old, just the age I was looking for, they were ready to find a forever home. They were called Glauten and Glieben, and I have absolutely no idea what the origins of those Germanic-sounding names are, but just 41 days after I lost my Nougat, Honey and Mustard became part of my household.

* * *

I digress a little. The growing feelings of anxiety were not something I was unfamiliar with. I had suffered bouts of anxiety and depression throughout my adult life but had always managed to come out the other side, usually with the help of some medication, counselling or indeed, hypnotherapy.

Since my last difficult phase, about six years previously, my GP had kept me on a lower dose of antidepressants as I had a history of relapses, and this had kept me on an even keel through some of my most challenging adventures, but when you've been there before you soon recognise the little signs that something isn't quite right. The previous two years had been like no others in my lifetime. I had lived on my own for many years. The difference with the pandemic situation was having to actively avoid close social contact. That had to be a factor.

Prague would also represent my first experience of post-Covid travel, with all its regulations and vaccine requirements. There were no direct flights available between Birmingham and Prague on our dates of travel, so Clare and I would fly via Munich on the way out, and Frankfurt on our return. This meant taking into account the rules and regulations of the UK, Germany and the Czech Republic, all of which seemed to change every few days.

I also had some concerns about leaving Honey and Mustard for the first time, even though it was only for four days. Through the winter months, after I brought them home, they had been kept indoors at all times, but as the warmer spring weather arrived they had enjoyed their first taste of freedom around the local neighbourhood. While I was away I planned to restrict them to the house once again, purely to save my cat-sitting neighbours the worry of them going missing. My rational brain told me that they would cope with being shut in again for just a few days, but my rampantly anxious brain threw up all sorts of unlikely scenarios for me to worry about.

And then perhaps the most important question of all: how was my running fitness? The simple answer was not that great. Apart from the relatively short periods out with my knee problem, and the head injury following my heavy fall, I had managed to keep running on the majority of days of the pandemic, although daily distances were usually around three to four miles. Even trying to run for six miles without stopping for a breather was proving very difficult; my endurance and self-confidence had undoubtedly suffered.

As the date of the Prague race grew closer at far too rapid a pace for my liking, I dragged myself around a ten-mile route with several laps around our lake. It was harder than I ever imagined. The advantage of running laps was that I could take on a drink and energy gel from my parked car at regular intervals on what was a pretty flat route but, even then, I was forced to walk most of the last mile. But, do you know what? That run convinced me that I could still run the Prague half-marathon.

I was now approaching my mid-70s and I knew that the vast majority of people of that age would give anything to be able to take on a challenge like that. Personal best times were now a decade or more in the past and I was at that happy running age when the only thing that mattered was enjoyment. What if it took me two and a half hours or more? I was about to run around a city I had never visited before, and add another location to my worldwide map.

* * *

Departure day arrived; it was time to take a deep breath and set out on the journey after a final few days full of unwanted surprises and uncertainty. True to form, there was a last-minute change of hotel as our original venue was still not open fully following the pandemic. It had seemed almost obligatory for this to happen on my recent running trips. A quick review of the city map showed that this should not really impact getting to the expo to pick up our race numbers, or indeed the start.

At one point it seemed that Clare and I would be landing in Prague at exactly the same time as Drew and Catharine were arriving from the States, via Heathrow. When looking at transport options from the airport into the city, a very reasonable option seemed to be sharing a limousine service between the four of us; we could arrive in Prague in style! The following day, Drew and Catharine's flight was cancelled, so that was another idea that went out of the window.

Online check-in also brought its own challenges. We were required to complete a passenger locator form for entry into the Czech Republic and I received an acknowledgement that mine met the necessary requirements; Clare heard nothing. The shoe was on the other foot when it came to submitting our vaccination status to our airline in order to confirm that we would be able to board. Clare was given the all-clear after they reviewed her documents but I heard nothing regarding mine. After a lengthy telephone call, the time mostly consumed by piped music, I was told they were too busy to respond to everybody and that I should just show up at check-in anyway; not what you want to hear when your anxiety is already running high.

The relief when we were told at the check-in desk that we were both good to go was immense. I used to enjoy the airport experience in previous years – not any more. The replacement of helpful, friendly faces with electronic gadgetry, and the constant feeling of being rushed and shouted at as you go through security, make it an altogether unpleasant experience. Nevertheless, we made it through, our flight to Munich was on time, and there was no turning back now. Arrival in Munich marked our entry into the European Union, and for the first time for both of us since Brexit we faced the ignominy of joining a lengthy immigration queue rather than being fast-tracked through as EU citizens.

The onward short flight to Prague on what seemed a rather flimsy aircraft was uneventful; the driver we had booked to replace the limousine was waiting for us, holding up a sheet of paper with my name on it as we entered the arrivals area and, by late afternoon, we were checked into our hotel. Given all the uncertainty and confusion of the previous few days, the journey itself could not have gone much more smoothly.

The same could not be said for poor Catharine and Drew. They had both been plagued by flight cancellations from their respective homes in the States to Heathrow, but in London at least they were able to meet up for a short while before their onward journey to Prague. Destiny, however, had it that they would not be on the same aircraft. Drew, who turns left at the cabin door when he travels, was able to get a flight that would reach Prague later in the evening of the same day that Clare and I had arrived. Catharine was not so lucky, and would have to spend a night in a Heathrow hotel before flying onwards the next day, losing one night of her hotel booking; the joys of post-Covid travel.

Just to rub salt into the wounds, although Drew finally arrived at our hotel late in the night of his scheduled date, his luggage did not. Even worse, Drew had made the cardinal error of not at least packing his running trainers in his hand luggage and now faced an anxious wait to see if his hold bag could be traced before race day, which was now only 36 hours away.

At least Liz and her sister Jenny had completed their trip successfully and had arrived in Prague the day before Clare and I. Jenny was not a runner but had come along to support us all and to visit a city she had never been to before.

* * *

So what happened next was like a bolt from the blue for me. Having checked in to our hotel, we met up with Liz and Jenny and walked to a nearby restaurant for a splendid chatty meal, catching up with Liz and getting to know Jenny. When we got back to the hotel for our promised welcome drinks, Drew was still on his way but we were able to FaceTime Catharine in London to find out the latest on her travel misfortunes. When we retired for the night, having agreed a time to meet for breakfast, my mood was one of relief that, so far at least, everything was going to plan.

My mood the following morning could not have been more different. I have suffered bouts of anxiety and depression episodically for most of my adult life, with lengthy periods of calm in between, but I had never felt quite as panicky as when I woke that morning after what had been a fitful night's sleep. My whole body was shaking uncontrollably and I was hyperventilating like crazy as I fought to re-establish some normality to my breathing. Every muscle in my body seemed to be weak and misfiring, and I couldn't even envisage getting out of bed, let alone running a half-marathon the following day.

Clare quickly recognised that something was not right and went downstairs to fetch me some coffee (there were no facilities in the room) and some dry food for breakfast as I was feeling quite nauseous and could certainly not tolerate anything cooked. She returned downstairs to enjoy breakfast with the others, which later in the morning included Catharine, while I remained in bed, trying to get a grip of my quivering body and mind. This had all the hallmarks of a full-on panic attack, which I had never experienced before in my life. I always considered myself a driven and determined person when it came to my running, never afraid to take on adventures that frankly scared me but, at that precise moment, I knew I had to make a decision to give myself a bit of breathing space.

It still pains me today to say that I decided to withdraw from the half-marathon. I have had to miss a few domestic races over the years through injury or illness, but this would be the very first time I had travelled abroad for a race and failed to make the start line. Even in Rio, when a sickness bug swept through our hotel in the days leading up to the half-marathon, I had managed to recover sufficiently not only to start the race, but also to finish, although in retrospect it may not have been the wisest decision.

When Clare checked on me after she had finished her breakfast, I told her my decision and she was totally understanding and supportive. Later that afternoon the plan was for our whole group to walk to the expo to pick up race numbers and our event T-shirts, and when I met everybody again in the hotel foyer, they could not have been more caring and sympathetic. Jenny had never intended to run anyway but had come along with her sister to support us all, and then Catharine also announced that she would not be running because of an ongoing knee injury, so we were down to three runners and three supporters – but it still felt great to have most of the Easter Island 'Band of Brothers' together again.

We walked together to the expo by a fairly circuitous route which included a brief visit to the city's impressive main railway station. Although my number would never be pinned to the front of my running vest, I still collected it along with the T-shirt I had paid for, and an extra free commemorative T-shirt, marking the return of the race following the two-year Covid delay.

Although my tremor was still very noticeable, my breathing had returned to normal and I was beginning to feel more settled. After a pleasant pasta meal together we returned to the hotel to find that Drew's luggage had still not arrived and the race was now only hours away. There was nothing else he could do but to go out on a late-evening shopping trip to buy new trainers and some kit to wear; it is never a good plan to run in new trainers for the first time in a race, but needs must. While the others in our party joined him, I remained in the hotel foyer with a beer, with a brief to message Drew should his luggage eventually arrive. Of course the inevitable happened. Just minutes before they all returned to the hotel with Drew's new purchases, a taxi driver wheeled his lost suitcase up to the reception desk. Money not so well spent but at least Drew could run in his own tried and tested gear.

* * *

Race day. After a light breakfast together, the support crew of Jenny, Catharine and myself saw our running trio off on their two-kilometre walk to the start and finish area in Jan Palach Square, named after the young political activist who had died by self-immolation in 1969, in protest at the Soviet invasion. Outside the temperature hovered around zero, there was a bitingly cold wind and snow flurries filled the air; tough conditions for Clare, Liz and Drew. A while later, our support crew began the same journey, but pausing at souvenir shops, street markets and finally a wine bar, if only for a brief respite from the cold.

Knowing that Clare was likely to be the first one home of our running trio, we found a gap at the spectator railings on the finishing straight, but only just in time. Almost immediately Clare came racing past us with sheer determination on her face, to the point where she didn't even hear our raucous cheers from the sidelines. A while later, first Liz and then Drew came through the finish, both acknowledging our ovation, and before too long we were all together again, three of the group proudly wearing their hard-earned medals. Somehow Clare had also managed to get a medal for me, but I knew it would sit in a drawer at home as a souvenir of a great trip with friends and would never be displayed with the couple of hundred others which I had shed blood, sweat, and sometimes tears for.

As expected, it had been a very tough race. The general consensus from our running trio was that, in such a beautiful city, the route might have been more appealing, with long sections on dual carriageways and around industrial estates; bitingly cold headwinds causing chapped lips added to the difficulty. Having said that, the sections in the city itself were very challenging too, with a mixture of cobbles and endless tram lines to negotiate. But all three had triumphed which, sadly, on this occasion, I had not.

* * *

Our final day together in Prague began with a sightseeing stroll around the Old Town, first joining a tour around the famous Klentinium complex, which not only housed the magnificent baroque Library Hall but also the astronomical clock tower with a display of 18th-century instruments used by some of the most famous astronomers of the time. With impeccable timing, we were able to get outside to join the hordes of tourists to watch the spectacle of the clock in action as the hour of 11 struck. In truth, it was a bit of an anti-climax. Bypassing the rather curious attraction of the Sex Machines Museum, we crossed the Vltava river over the iconic Charles Bridge, its magnificent statues and history offering so many photo opportunities.

Now it was time to meet up with Vladimir, our guide on an afternoon food tour that Liz had pre-arranged for us. It gave us a chance to visit six of Prague's lesser-known restaurants, pubs and delicatessens, and to sample the food and drink on offer. From roast duck to pastries, the tour was so much more than just a taster session. Vladimir was an engaging and knowledgeable host who answered just about every question we could think of regarding the city's food, culture, people, politics or history. It was a fitting end to our time together although it may just have had one final consequence that would play out the following day.

The next morning, it was time to say goodbye to our American friends as we each made our respective journeys home, although Drew planned to spend a few days in London on a tour of West End theatre productions. However, a troubled but enjoyable trip had one final sting in the tail. On the second leg of our flight back home, between Frankfurt and Birmingham, poor Clare became suddenly and violently ill. I will spare the full details but suffice to say that some rows of seating in the cabin had to be evacuated and the occupants unexpectedly found themselves moved to business class on a pretty full aircraft.

Once on the ground, we were quickly ushered past the long immigration queues at Birmingham, although Clare was still being ill when we met her brother who was giving us a lift back to our homes. Indeed, Clare spent the next four days in bed and lost an awful lot of weight. Was it food poisoning from our tour with Vladimir? None of the rest of us seemed to have been affected, although it was hard to find any other explanation that could have caused such a violent, sudden, and indeed, prolonged illness.

* * *

So, from a personal point of view, how would I sum up the Prague trip? For the very first time in my whole running life I had travelled abroad for a race and not even made the start line, let alone the finish. I had questions to ask of myself, but was I in the right frame of mind to answer them yet? With the travel and fitness anxieties now behind me, my expectation on returning home was that my mindset would return to normal, whatever that was for me. Sadly this turned out not to be the case and the anxiety and depression deepened further. Was it the sense of failure I was feeling?

I had been through times like this before in my life, and I had come out the other side. I could do it again. I knew that I might need some help in the shorter term so self-referred to a counselling service, and dug out some old hypnotherapy session recordings that had helped me in the past.

I tried to get an appointment with my local GP surgery, but in post-Covid times this was becoming increasingly difficult. When you are struggling with anxiety already, there is nothing more anxiety-inducing than being told on several occasions to phone the surgery first thing the next morning, only to be told then that there were still no appointments available. Eventually, I managed to secure a telephone appointment and was able to get a temporary increase in the dose of my usual anxiety medication. Support from friends and family was also an immense comfort. There does seem to be a much wider understanding of mental wellbeing issues these days than there had been in the past. In fact, around this time, several elite sporting personalities, from a variety of sports, were being very open about their own wellbeing difficulties. Whatever our levels of performance, we had together been through the most unsettling couple of years of our lifetimes. It was a comfort to know I was not alone.

The days passed by in similar fashion, but I could feel a very gradual improvement over time and, from past experience, knew that recovery was not going to happen suddenly. Even as I put pen to paper now (metaphorically, of course) a few months on there are still bumps in the road, but it is slowly heading in the right direction. Apart from the odd occasion, which was usually accompanied by anxiety dreams, I would sleep well but then wake in fear of the day ahead. This feeling would gradually dissipate as the day unfolded until, by bedtime, I would be feeling pretty much like the normal Doug, only for the morning anxiety cycle to be repeated the following day. One thing helped consistently: going for a run lifted my mood, even if it was only for a mile or two.

With endurance still being a bit of a mental issue, I adopted a new running regime of running more regularly but keeping the runs shorter. By doing this, I was not only getting a more frequent mental boost but I could still log around 100 miles a month, and was now edging ever closer to one of my lifetime goals. You may recall that in the first chapter of this book, I had set myself the long-term target of running the distance of the circumference of our world, 24,902 miles. At the time that was 5,000 miles away, but now I was approaching the final few hundred miles. I was close enough to dare thinking about how I was going to celebrate that milestone, but far enough away to not want to tempt fate.

But even in the more challenging times, running still had the ability to shine a shaft of light into what, on occasions, seemed to be endless gloom. In mid-April, an unexpected email revealed that I had been selected to take part in the Queen's Baton Relay in the lead-up to the Commonwealth Games, which were to be held in the neighbouring city of Birmingham. What an honour! I knew that I had been nominated by a fellow runner of a similar vintage, Alan, but with nominations exceeding the places available by several times I felt truly privileged to be one of the lucky ones chosen. My opportunity would come during late July, and now I had yet another great incentive to reset my current frame of mind in a more positive direction.

Chapter 11

Snakes, ladders and hope

SO WHAT exactly is the Queen's Baton Relay and, for the benefit of many of my overseas readers, what is the Commonwealth, or more accurately, the Commonwealth of Nations? Let's start with the latter. Harking back to the controversial days of the British empire, and the colonisation of overseas territories, the current Commonwealth was instigated in 1949 and is an association of 56 member states, the great majority of which were former territories of the empire. All member states are now 'free and equal', the majority are republics, just five have their own monarchs and Queen Elizabeth II was, at the time, the current head of state of the remainder. Every four years, a different country of the Commonwealth hosts a multi-sport celebration, the Commonwealth Games, akin to the Olympic Games but only open to the 56 member states. These had become known as the 'Friendly Games' and, for 2022, had been awarded to the city of Birmingham, just a dozen or so miles from my front door.

As a prelude to the Games, a baton relay takes place through each of the 56 Commonwealth nations, as well as 16 additional territories, before the baton is finally delivered to the head of the Commonwealth, or their representative, at the opening ceremony, in a similar fashion to the Olympic torch relay. I would now be part of that historic journey. On 7 October 2021 at Buckingham Palace, the Queen, as the current head of the Commonwealth, placed a message inside the baton and it began its journey around the 72 states and territories.

Designed and manufactured in the West Midlands, the baton itself was largely constructed of readily accessible metals – copper, aluminium and brass – but with a thin strand of platinum running through it to mark the Queen's Platinum Jubilee year. Within the casing, apart from the message, was a whole range of gadgetry: a 360-degree camera, LED lighting, a monitor recording the heart rate of the baton bearer, and environmental conditions sensors, sampling the air as it travelled around the globe.

When the relay route and timings were announced for the West Midlands region, with a few weeks to go to the big day, I was initially a little disappointed to find myself allocated to a location some 50 miles from home. Don't get me wrong; I would have travelled anywhere to fulfil that great honour, but I had expected to be a little more local so that more of my friends and family could share the moment with me. However, as time drew nearer, I received a phone call from the relay organisers, asking if I minded switching my leg to the borough of Solihull, just a 20-minute drive from my home. My turn would come just two days before the opening ceremony; I didn't need asking twice!

* * *

But back to the running for now. Edging ever closer was the Iceland Volcano half-marathon, a race I had entered almost three years earlier in very different times, and indeed, with a very different mindset going on between my ears. My struggles with the anxiety issues were proving harder to overcome than I had anticipated from my previous experiences, despite the help I was getting. It was more of a roller-coaster ride than a steady return to pre-lockdown Doug. Yes, there were good days when I believed I was finally turning the corner, but then, out of the blue, the angst would rise up again, and knock me back a few pegs, like a game of snakes and ladders.

The memories of what I perceived to be a failure in Prague were still fresh in my mind, despite the passing of a few months. The first goal I had set myself on my running recovery plan was to enter a race I knew I could physically complete, if I could just banish the mental negativities that I knew would arise. I entered a 10km race in nearby Evesham, about half an hour away from where I live, and a race I had run several years previously.

I always get butterflies in my stomach before a race; that is normal for me. For goodness sake, I even feel a bit fretful before a parkrun, and I had run several hundred

Running the Serra Tronquiera forest trails. (credit: Dave Gratton)

Atlantic spotted dolphins enjoying their freedom in the seas off the coast of Sao Miguel Island.

Julie and I enjoying the crowd support as we run through St Mark's Square in the closing stages of the Venice Marathon. (credit: Pica)

Mission accomplished! Crossing the finish line of the Venice Marathon with Julie. (credit: Pica)

Mike's 'Team Venice' runners celebrating their achievements. Back row, (left to right): Peter, Julie, me, Adam, Jon. Front row, (left to right): Richard, Caroline, Stuart, Mike.

A Venetian sunset

With Paul, preparing to set off for the opening time-trial of the Cyprus 4-day Challenge. (credit: Kevin Fernandes)

The closing stages of the time-trial with the rusting wreck of Edro III *in the background. (credit: Kevin Fernandes)*

Celebrating completion of the Cyprus 4-day Challenge with a plastic cup of beer. (credit: Kevin Fernandes)

My trophy and medal haul from the Cyprus 4-day Challenge.

The presentation of my age category award for the Bermuda Triangle Challenge from a government minister, taking care not to spill my rum cocktail in my other hand.

Post-race celebrations after the Bermuda 10km race with some of the Gombey dancers (left to right): Lynn, Liz, me, Peg.

So what exactly could have happened to the Bermuda Triangle tram?

Receiving the Queen's Baton from my forerunner, Angela.

Enjoying every moment of my 200 metre segment carrying the Queen's Baton – one of the proudest moments of my life.

Preparing to embark on the final 5km equator run with son, Chris, helium balloons of the planet at the ready.

The moment a lifetime goal was completed: running the length of the equator, 24,902 miles.

Celebrating with parkrun friends – it was Halloween weekend if you are concerned about the appearance of some!!!

of those. This was one of those races where you would pick up your race number on the day itself, and this caused me a few quite irrational concerns. What if I couldn't find somewhere close to park? How long would the queue be for picking up our numbers and would I still have time to fill in my emergency contact details on the back of the number, and then pin it to my running vest? I sometimes wish I could be like those who turn up at the last minute, magically find the last available parking space, and are still pinning on their number as the race starts, but that is not me. I have to be ultra early and as prepared as I can possibly be.

I appreciate that these mind meanderings may seem absurd to some, but I just want to convey to my readers, and particularly those who don't suffer from anxiety, how my mind was working at the time. Anyway, redemption was at hand. Just two days before the race itself I received an email telling me I could pick up my number the evening before. This did mean an extra round trip to Evesham but gave me the opportunity to recce parking areas, the layout of the race village and, of course, pick up my number to take home, so that I could fill in the information and attach it to my race vest at leisure. Believe me, that really made such a difference.

The following day, I completed the Evesham 10k. It was an uncomfortably warm day, on a mixed-terrain course, but I ran every step, apart from two short stops at the much-needed water stations. When my race medal was hung around my neck, I knew that this had been a small but significant pushback on my Prague experience.

* * *

Tuesday, 26 July 2022: the day I would carry the Queen's Baton. I had been allocated to a segment in Hockley Heath, a village within the borough of Solihull. Each segment was about 200 metres long, so the distance would be no problem for me! Some weeks before, I had been sent my uniform of a pink and white, long-sleeved shirt, emblazoned with the motifs of the Commonwealth Games and the Queen's Baton Relay, and it had hung untouched in my wardrobe since then. When the big day arrived, Chris and Cam dropped me off at a school in Temple Balsall which was the designated meeting point for several of the baton bearers who would be fulfilling their dream around Solihull that afternoon.

Having checked in with the organisers, and having my identity confirmed, I was able to spend some time with some of the other baton bearers, and we shared our stories of how we had each managed to arrive at that point. There were so many inspirational tales of people who go above and beyond in their routine daily lives. After a detailed briefing of what lay ahead of us, we were then transported to the beginning of our segments. Most travelled by coach, but the five of us running through Hockley Heath were taken by minibus to our designated lamp-posts, through streets lined with expectant spectators. As I was dropped off at lamp-post 101 – I was the 101st baton bearer that day – we were under strict instructions not to move an inch from our drop-off point, as the full procession was by now only about two segments behind us. There was just enough time for a few quick photos with friends before the motorcycle outriders of the main procession came into view.

The organisation of the Baton Relay was a truly complex operation with a huge amount of security involved. As the convoy approached, I was ushered by a member of the police security team into the centre of the road and surrounded by a posse of more police in orange and white Commonwealth Games uniforms, where I received the baton from my forerunner, Angela. We paused briefly for a few official handover photos and then I broke into a slow – and I really mean slow – jog. I was going to make this last as long as possible.

It was such an emotional 200 metres of running. The crowd were several deep on both sides of the road, and the noise that they made was deafening. It was lovely to see so many children waving flags and cheering, and it was great to have had so many of my family and friends there, to share the special moment with me. The baton weighed 1.6kg and it was beginning to feel quite heavy as I held it aloft above my head. As I reached the end of my segment, the security team, in turn, shook my hand, and then took the baton from me as it was now due to travel by road on to the next village, Dickens Heath.

It was one of the proudest moments of my life and a day I will never forget. Just two days later, I watched on my TV screen as the Queen's Baton reached the end of its journey, and was handed to the Duchess of Cornwall at the Commonwealth Games Opening Ceremony. I had a tear in my eye to think that I had been entrusted with its safekeeping for those precious few minutes.

* * *

As a footnote to this most memorable of days, almost four months after the event itself, each of the baton bearers received a replica baton, one-third the size of the original, and individually engraved with our names and details of the segment we had run; a wonderful keepsake of one of the proudest moments of my life.

* * *

On the very same Saturday as the opening ceremony, it happened to be my 400th parkrun and I was eager to give my pink and white long-sleeved shirt another celebratory outing. A wonderful running friend of mine of a similar vintage, Peggy, who was on finish tokens that morning, had also had the honour of carrying the baton the day after me, in Birmingham. Neither of us had had the opportunity to share each other's big day, so we agreed to meet up at parkrun in our uniforms so that we could at least get a photo together.

Precious moments like these were beginning to restore the self-confidence and belief that I enjoyed in the pre-lockdown era. Yes, there would still be some difficult days ahead but, little by little, I was edging in a more positive direction. In my eyes it was very noticeable that it wasn't only me whose running had been affected by the two years of social avoidance. Many people in my own running groups, who had been regular attendees before the pandemic, didn't return when restrictions were lifted and attendances at our local parkrun were significantly lower than the pre-Covid days.

* * *

Just a month before the Iceland trip, in Solihull another 10k was scheduled and offered a further opportunity for me to enjoy a race day experience. I was much more familiar with the layout of the town than I had been with Evesham, as I had run its Brueton parkrun on several occasions in the past. Nevertheless, I still visited the race village and start area the day before the race just to see how long it would take me to walk there from where I usually parked my car. It all helped me to soothe the nerves on the day itself.

The routes of the 10k, and indeed the half-marathon which was being run concurrently, were described as undulating. Anyone who has ever run a race with that description will know that this is a less off-putting term for hilly! In the days leading up to the race, temperatures in the Midlands were beginning to soar again, prompting the Met Office to issue heatwave warnings, with a peak expected on the day itself. The organisers seemed reluctant to add extra water stations en route, inviting participants to carry their own water instead, and this prompted several of those who had entered the half-marathon to transfer to the shorter distance. With temperatures expected to hit the mid-30s Celsius, I decided to wear a half-filled Camelbak with plenty of ice cubes floating within it, and this proved to be a sensible decision on a challenging day. Yes, I did walk up a couple of the steeper hills, and my finish time was a few minutes slower than at Evesham, but when the medal was hung around my neck I knew I had taken another small step in the right direction.

* * *

Let me say right here and now that I feel utterly privileged to have visited the many parts of our world that my running adventures have taken me to. One of the most common questions that I am asked when I give one of my running travel talks, is, 'Do I have sponsors who pay for these trips?' The answer is no. For me, they are my holidays and I pay every penny myself.

I am not particularly someone who enjoys lying on a sunny beach or beside a hotel pool. Having spent the majority of my running years as a single person, I at least do not have the additional expense of taking a running or non-running partner with me, and this has helped to make the trips more affordable.

One way I have been able to give something back for the amazing experiences I have enjoyed has been to use my adventure runs as a means for raising money for charity, by getting people, and occasionally businesses, to boost my charity coffers. If you are one of those people who has waded through my two previous books, and are now close to completing the trilogy, you will know that I have raised many tens of thousands of pounds for a variety of charities over the years, and this is something I am immensely proud of.

But, for the first time in my memory, I had made the decision not to fundraise on my Iceland Volcano trip, purely to ease the pressure on myself at a time when my mental fortitude was still fragile. Usually I would have contacted the local papers, radio stations and TV to widen the circle of publicity, and hopefully boost the charity funds further, but this run was going to be for me; just me.

* * *

And then it happened again! In the early hours of the day before our departure panic attack number two struck, and it was truly quite frightening. The sweating, the racing heartbeat, the relentless shaking and the fast and rapid breathing; it was just not possible to get it under control. I tried to see if I could sleep through it but that was futile. I got up, paced around the house, drank lots of water as if that would provide a magic cure, but I didn't want to take in any caffeine that might increase my heart rate further.

I remembered that I still had a single tablet of the low dose of diazepam I had been given after my previous panic attack and took that, but how long would it be before it had any effect? The night seemed to go on forever. I knew I needed some medical advice but was in no condition to drive myself anywhere, so opted to phone my GP surgery as soon as it opened at 8.30am to book a telephone appointment. I knew I had to let Clare, my travelling partner, know what was going on, so I waited for a respectable hour, knowing that she was an early riser anyway, before messaging her. Clare and Bill live less than half a mile from me and, true to her caring nature, she was soon knocking on my front door to make sure I wasn't going to present any danger to myself. Having satisfied herself of that, and in the knowledge that I would speak to a doctor later that day, Clare reassured me that whatever the outcome of that discussion I should do what was right for me and not take into account the consequences it would have on her own trip. Running friends are the best.

When the call from the doctor finally came through, I already knew in my heart that this was going to be another running adventure that wasn't going to happen. While he could not forbid me from going, it was very clear that I would be taking an enormous risk travelling to a distant country in the state I was in, and even my own muddled brain knew that I would be putting an onerous burden on Clare's shoulders should I decide to continue with the trip. I was prescribed the maximum safe dose of diazepam to take for the following few days.

I contacted Clare to let her know and I told my immediate family that I wouldn't be climbing that volcano after all. Indeed, I even mentioned that this might mark the point when I would have to call it a day on my foreign running adventures. I felt desolate. I was at the tip of the tail of the longest snake on the anxiety game board.

* * *

It wasn't just Clare who I felt I had let down, but also her husband Bill. He had entrusted me with keeping her company on a challenging trip, as he had done in the past, but now she would be travelling solo. But Clare is nothing if not resolute, and I am delighted to report that she completed the trip and the half-marathon, making new running friends along the way, and even found the time to send me daily updates and photos of what I was missing. On her return, Clare even offered to repeat the trip in 2023 if I felt well enough to do it then, but that was a decision a long way ahead – if it were to happen at all.

In the meantime, I had some more immediate choices to make regarding the future direction of my running journey. Physically, I was still in pretty good shape for a guy in his mid-70s. This was exemplified by an amusing exchange of emails from a group of gentlemen known as the 'Class of '59'. Back in 1959, as 11-year-olds, we had all started our grammar school education at the same time. Now spread across the world, many of us had met up in Brighton in 2014 for a reunion and a chance to look around our old school. One of our group had raised the possibility of another reunion in 2023 to celebrate reaching three-quarters of a century. In discussing what venue we might meet at, one of the points raised was accessibility, with one of my former schoolmates, now living in Canada, uttering the classic words, 'We're not all bloody Doug Richards, you know!'

While my number one reason for running was, and will always be, enjoyment, the Covid lockdown period had seen my endurance suffer, and the last half-marathon I had completed had been the one in Bermuda in the very earliest days of the pandemic. Don't get me wrong, I have absolutely no doubt that if I started out on a half-marathon race I would get to the finish line, however long it took, but would it be an enjoyable experience? Just maybe the time had come, in my current situation at least, to set my distance goals a little lower, but leaving the option open if my mental wellbeing were to improve in the future.

The first decision I made was to abandon any plans to complete the ill-fated Superhalfs series, for the time being at least. Prague had been destined to be my first of the five events, and I knew the chances of me returning there to have another go, without the support and encouragement of my running friends around me, were remote. I also had an entry for Cardiff, another race in the series, but was able to transfer that to a local friend of mine, Carina. For now, or at least until I started to feel more confident in myself, 10km or thereabouts would be my distance, because I knew that I could finish that with a smile on my face.

* * *

On 8 September 2022, Her Majesty Queen Elizabeth II passed away, and the connection I felt having carried her baton just seven weeks previously deepened my sorrow as the country entered a period of mourning. My own son, Chris, was heavily involved as a Royal Air Force drill instructor in the preparations for the Queen's funeral to be held on 19 September, and this gave me a unique insight into the enormous amount of work that went in to making such state occasions unfold seamlessly on the day.

I sat and watched every minute of the service on television, from both London and Windsor, as I have enormous respect for the Queen's service over her lifetime, but the general mourning engulfing the country did little to lift my own mood. A particularly significant low came the Saturday morning after the funeral, when I woke and couldn't face the prospect of going to parkrun. Other than having some unavoidable engagement, or being ill or injured, parkrun is a key part of my weekly routine, and one of the few times of the week when I was guaranteed good social interaction, but I was weepy and shaky and didn't want my friends to see me like that so I stayed in bed. I regretted it later.

* * *

But over the following days and weeks, a few key jigsaw pieces began to drop into place. After many months on the waiting list for some counselling, I was informed that I had finally reached the top and would shortly begin a course of cognitive behavioural therapy.

I also knew, in my own mind, that the drug treatment I had been getting since the first panic attack in Prague was simply not working and, if anything, it was making me feel worse with its unwanted side effects. Whether it's a good thing or a bad thing, I knew that I had far more scientific knowledge about what was going on inside my brain than the average patient. After all, my doctorate had studied the biochemical changes occurring in psychiatric illness, I had edited a textbook about disorders of the brain and their treatment, and I had taught medical students about the mechanisms behind psychoactive drugs. Indeed, some of the GPs at my own surgery were former students of mine. I had gone along with the advice that doubling the dose of my existing medication was the way forward, and was repeatedly told so by different GPs on each prescription renewal call, but now was the time to stand up for myself and demand some change.

I would never knock the National Health Service, having worked in it for over 20 years, and also knowing many people still working within it under the most demanding conditions brought on by the pandemic and its aftermath, but I think all would agree that GP services were not as easily accessible as they were beforehand when it was quite simple to make an appointment with a GP who knew you and your past medical history. The system operating at our health centre, for non-urgent care, was to go online at exactly 8.30am when a list of available telephone appointments with various doctors would be made available, and to book one as quickly as you could as they would be snapped up within minutes, and then you would be forced to have to wait until the following day to try again.

On the day in question, I sat poised over my keyboard. At the promised hour a list popped up and, near the top, I saw a few appointments with a senior partner who I had seen once or twice over the 25 years I had been registered with the practice. I clicked on one of the appointment times, quickly typed 'ongoing anxiety' into the 'reason for appointment' box, pressed 'book', only to be told that someone had beaten me to that slot! I growled with frustration; this was not a good system for someone who was already suffering from anxiety. I returned to the original list, scrolled down a list of GPs who I had never heard of previously, and there, at the very bottom was the man who I would describe as my own GP, who had known me and my history for many years. He had two appointments available. I chose one, didn't bother to fill in the 'reason' box, and pressed 'book'. Success. I would receive a telephone call from a doctor who I trusted and who knew me well later that day. The relief was just so intense.

When he did call, he readily agreed that a new approach to medication was needed, and we made appointments for a face-to-face meeting and for some blood tests to see if there was anything that might explain my failure to respond in the preceding six months. Was this the turning point I was looking for?

* * *

To cut a long story short, the answer to that question was 'quite possibly'. The blood tests revealed no abnormalities other than very low vitamin D levels, which could be easily rectified by taking daily supplements. As many may be aware, changing one antidepressant for another is not a speedy process in order to avoid some pretty unpleasant withdrawal effects. Over a period of weeks the daily dose of my original medication was progressively lowered to a minimum, at which point a low dose of the new substance was introduced. This period of time for me was running parallel to my cognitive behavioural therapy sessions, which took place over the telephone and online and were changing the way I was thinking about my worries. Indeed, they taught me that some of the techniques I had been using myself may actually have been exacerbating my problems.

By the middle of October I was waking in the morning and not feeling that tight knot of butterflies in my stomach, and that initial dread of the day ahead. In the previous six months there had been days when I had woken like this, but the relief had been temporary and the apprehension and loss of confidence had soon returned. Now I was sustaining this more positive outlook for days at a time. There were more measurable signs of improvement too. With a past history of blood pressure problems I routinely check my readings every few days anyway. For months these had been noticeably higher than they usually were, but now they had returned to pre-pandemic levels. Similarly with my weight; the seven to ten pounds that had dropped off after my Prague panic attack now gradually crept back on as my appetite improved, bringing me back to what I considered to be a normal healthy weight for me.

There were improvements on the running front as well. Out of nowhere, I suddenly produced two consecutive parkrun times that were a good two or three minutes quicker than I had been achieving for months. OK, they were a long way from the elusive personal best days, but they were a beacon of hope. I was arriving at parkrun with a spring in my step and a smile on my face rather than sitting in my car until the last minute to limit the amount of social interaction I felt I would have to endure. Little by little, the clouds were slowly parting and the sun was beginning to peep through again.

It really couldn't have happened at a better time for, despite all the gloomy times of the preceding months, the best medicine for me continued to be that regular boost I felt from even a short run outdoors, and now a huge personal milestone had crept into touching distance. I was about to complete one lap of the planet.

Chapter 12

You can Dough it!

EVEN BEFORE these green shoots of recovery were beginning to emerge, I was acutely aware that my long-term goal of running the length of the equator was going to be reached sooner or later, and I had started to plan in my mind how best to celebrate it. Even in my darkest moments I wouldn't have wanted to have reached that milestone on a lonely solo run. The support of my running friends had kept me going through some very challenging times and I had made several of them aware of the upcoming landmark.

In the end, I decided that there was only one place that met all the requirements for my celebratory plans, and that was my local Arrow Valley parkrun. As my running log entered the final 100 miles, and knowing roughly the mileage I could reasonably expect to complete in the interim period, I set 29 October 2022 as my target date. I let our local core team of volunteers know of my plans as each week, at the pre-run briefing, we celebrate those reaching the official parkrun milestone achievements (10, 25, 50, 100 and 250), whether they be for participating or volunteering, and I didn't want those to be overshadowed by a non-parkrun-related goal.

There were other considerations too. In the true spirit of parkrun, celebratory events were often completed in fancy dress. What would be an appropriate costume for an equator run? I did trawl the internet and come up with one rotund planet earth outfit, but it looked to be almost impossible to run in without causing serious damage to those around me. In the end, I settled for a more measured approach with a customised T-shirt showing a two-dimensional map of the world on the front, with the equator drawn across it, while attached to my waist, and hovering above my head would be a large spherical helium balloon of our wonderful world.

Did I want to publicise the run to the wider local community? While there was no fundraising planned for this particular milestone, it was nevertheless a significant personal achievement and I knew it would be of interest to many of my local friends for whom running had no attraction whatsoever. You may recall that in the lead-up to my aborted Iceland trip, I had avoided any media contact because I knew it would just add an extra layer of pressure at the time, but now the clouds of anxiety were beginning to disperse I did notify my local newspapers and radio station of my plan. To say I was taken aback by the response would be an understatement; my equator achievement certainly grabbed plenty of media attention at a time when most of the news was making pretty grim reading.

My running during the final week leading up to the big day had to be quite carefully scheduled. The plan was that I would reach the magic target of 24,902 miles just as I reached the parkrun finish line. What I didn't want to do was to accidentally reach that goal beforehand with one of my running groups or perhaps on a couch to 5k session. The tailored runs were fitted in between an increasingly busy media schedule; it was interesting to see how news spreads through the media and I was contacted by several print and radio outlets who I had not notified previously. I even had the pleasure of hosting a BBC local radio team as they broadcast from my own home, rummaging through my race medal collection and other running memorabilia.

One amusing little side story that arose from all this media attention was when one local newspaper posted an online article about the upcoming run, but added an 'h' to my first name, referring to me as Dough! My full first name of course is Douglas, although I always associate that with my dear mum calling me out when I may have transgressed into the realms of naughtiness. Nevertheless, aside from some frustration at modern-day journalistic standards, this unique spelling of my name caused a good deal of hilarity among my friends and family, and may be something I will have to live with for some time to come as the revised spelling became something of a personal trademark on social media posts.

When Friday eventually arrived, I carefully ran a measured couple of miles to leave just the magic five kilometres of parkrun remaining. I have to say that my stomach was tingling with excitement at the thought of what lay ahead the following morning. It had been far too many months since I had felt that almost childlike anticipation and I felt so relieved that the turnaround in my mindset had arrived at just the right time.

I had ordered four of the helium balloons from a local fancy dress shop: one for me, one for Chris, who would be joining me on my equator run, and two to be attached to the traffic cones that marked the finish line of our parkrun. As I arrived at the shop after my top-up run, I was initially dismayed to see a long queue stretching out from the doorway. It was Halloween weekend after all and business was brisk. When my turn finally came, and I was presented with the four large balloons by the manageress, who was aware of the reason that I had asked for them, she announced to the whole shop the landmark I would be achieving the following morning and I emerged to the sounds of applause and cheering, with the widest of grins on my face.

* * *

And so the big day arrived. After securing the two balloons to the finish line, Chris and I made our way to the amphitheatre area where the weekly pre-race briefing would take place. With gathering clouds threatening to put a dampener on proceedings, the assembled masses of runners, walkers and volunteers included a Grim Reaper, a selection of menacing ghosts and ghouls, and various suspicious-looking characters in bloodstained clothing. It all helped create a somewhat surreal atmosphere.

After acknowledging the official parkrun milestones, including my friend Peter, who was about to embark on his 250th run, our event director's wife Rachel caught me a bit by surprise by reading out a message I had sent to her, which explained just why I wanted this special personal moment to take place among parkrun friends who I really did hold dear to my heart, and who had been by my side through some pretty tough times.

With a little bit of wetness in my eyes, we began the 200-metre walk to the start line in readiness for my equator run. Some of my close friends, who would normally expect to finish their parkrun a little slower than me, had chosen not to run on this occasion just so that they could be at the finish line to witness my moment of triumph, and it touched me that they were prepared to do that. A few of my overseas running friends had expressed regret on social media that they couldn't attend the occasion, so Chris had agreed to broadcast the start and finish on Facebook Live with his phone. The wonders of modern technology.

A whistle sounded and we were set on our way. As with any parkrun start, there was a good deal of congestion in the early stages, and Chris and I fought to keep our tethered balloons close at hand so that following runners didn't get an unwanted faceful of our planet, but once the field was more spread out the balloons were released to the full extent of their ribbons. Many of my running friends who might normally expect to be a little faster than me over the five-kilometre route chose, this time, to run alongside me as we made our way around two laps of the lake and it was also warming to pass and acknowledge some of my non-running local friends who had taken the trouble to come out and be part of the occasion.

As we neared the finish, Chris pushed on ahead so that he could be in a good position to film the closing stages. I made the final turn and could see the finish line 100 metres ahead. I stepped up the pace amid a cacophony of cheering and shouting. The support I was getting carried me towards my goal. Our two globe balloons at the finish had been joined by two further inflatable Earths, and the finish funnel had been decorated with the flags of countries around the world.

I crossed the line. I stopped my watch. I had run once around the planet.

The following few minutes were just something of a euphoric blur. Casting aside all the pandemic inhibitions of the preceding two-plus years, I was prepared to hug anybody who wanted a hug. Selfies were taken with my closest buddies, and some with people I barely knew, and then we posed for great group photos with many of my dearest friends; runners and non-runners alike.

Once the formalities of registering my time had been completed, and the volunteer tail walkers behind the last finisher had crossed the line, we adjourned to the park cafe area where I was presented with a bottle of bubbly by our parkrun core team to mark the occasion. Even as my mind was beginning to process what I had finally achieved, another call came through from a radio station eager to hear my immediate reaction and, as I stood outside the cafe to speak to them, the rain finally began to fall.

* * *

So what comes next after you have finally completed a lap of the planet? Well, in my case, it was to start my lap of honour as I was booked to run a 10km race the following morning in my home town of Redditch. It was all part of the progress I felt I was gradually making as the true me slowly emerged from the preceding months of gloom. That voice in my head which had repeatedly told me 'I can't' was now not only saying 'I can', but also adding 'I will'. The race around Redditch was tough, particularly with an uphill final mile, but I crossed the line with a smile on my face and I couldn't ask for more than that. That was the first six miles ticked off on my second lap!

The response to my equator achievement had been far, far greater than I ever imagined, and it did get me thinking about just how many other people might have achieved that goal without realising it. Maybe it was the scientific and data-handling gene within me that had led me to be so fastidious with my record keeping, right from day one of my running career. These days running apps, such as Strava, will keep cumulative mileage records for you, so we may find in the years ahead that those who manage to run the distance of the equator during their running life are rather more common than we might otherwise imagine. In the meantime, I remained happy to reflect in the glory of the achievement!

An example of just how newsworthy my feat was being seen as came a couple of days after the event when I received an email from an individual whose name I did not recognise, asking simply if it was true that I had run the length of the equator. When I replied in the affirmative, the sender revealed herself to be a television documentary producer based in California. It emerged that she was researching prior to filming a documentary that would review a variety of facts and myths about the equator, this imaginary line that circles our planet. The lady was not a runner herself, and was amazed that anybody could have run that far, even given the length of time it had taken. We agreed to hold a Zoom chat at which we talked about my working career background, as well as many of the races I have done in the past and what motivated me to keep going in my later years. It was mentioned that it might be fun to film me running on the equator itself, possibly in Ecuador, although no mention was made of how such a trip might be financed. As I write I still await further developments, although it does seem that my story will feature in the documentary in some form which has given another boost to my ongoing self-confidence rebuild.

* * *

Excuse me now while I fetch my crystal ball and try to second guess what the future might hold for me with regard to running. In 2023 the number that defines me in so many people's eyes, my age, will reach three-quarters of a century. I don't feel that old, but none of us are guaranteed that tomorrow will come, and we live with the certain knowledge that there is a limit to how many tomorrows there will be. If I look in the rear-view mirror I see wonderful decades of running in all parts of the world and in all sorts of climatic conditions. I feel honoured and privileged to have achieved so much adventure in my lifetime but, even at this later stage, I still prefer to look forward.

Right now, my physical health can be described as good for my age, and my mental wellbeing continues to be moving in a more positive direction following the recent medication review. The only downside to the new regime is that it has currently led to rather more weight gain than I would have liked, but that is manageable although I certainly notice it when running uphill! On balance, a little more poundage is a small price to pay for the more positive mental outlook.

Having experienced false dawns previously, I have been keen not to push myself too hard, too soon, in my quest to get myself back to what I judge to be an acceptable level of personal fitness, taking into account the consequences of advancing years. For the remainder of 2022 I had decided that 10km would be my distance limit, but in the year that followed, could I get myself back to completing half-marathon races in a time that satisfied me personally? I'm not talking about setting unrealistic time targets that might warrant punishing training schedules to achieve, but rather something that fulfilled my inner competitiveness, and that would still leave a grin, and not a grimace, on my face at the finish line.

There remain two outstanding overseas trips that I had previously registered for and dearly want to undertake. Both are of half-marathon distance, although the terrain and likely weather conditions are such that the time taken would be irrelevant, and completion would be the only goal. The Madagascar race is provisionally scheduled for May 2023 but that has still to be confirmed at the time of writing. With the event having already been repeatedly postponed by the pandemic, the country itself has been affected by climate change more than most, resulting in widespread famine, and has seen much subsequent civil unrest. It may be that runner safety is a factor in the delay in confirming the race. Time will tell.

And then I have unfinished business with the Hverfjall volcano in Iceland. The next event is now scheduled for August 2023, and after the disappointment of missing out on my 2022 trip with Clare, I can feel a renewed determination that I am not going to let that happen again.

If, and it is a big 'if', I could complete those two target races, then just maybe I would have to take another look at the Superhalfs series. I could run Cardiff in October 2023, which would leave me two years to complete the other four cities. As an added bonus, two of my close running friends, Carina and Pauline, have already embarked on their own Superhalf journeys, so the prospect of having travelling companions for future races is looking bright.

Peering deeper into the crystal ball, another lifetime running goal that might potentially be reached towards the end of 2024, would be my wearing of the coveted blue '500 parkruns' T-shirt. I have said it before, and I will say it again – since my very first parkrun in the summer of 2012, shortly after returning from my rather traumatic, angry elephant experience in South Africa, this free weekly community event has enhanced my life and friendships more than I can ever explain, and I know the same applies to so many others. If the day ever comes when my legs won't carry me round the 5km route any more then you will see me there as a volunteer, or as a spectator, just so that I can be part of it.

* * *

So there we have it: 2022, a year of two enormously memorable moments with the baton bearing and equator runs, and two major disappointments with foreign adventures in Prague and Iceland. In between were some of the toughest times mentally I have endured for many years, but it is worthy of note that there was also 1,000 miles of running achieved during the year and, without that outlet, things could have been a whole lot worse for me.

As I draw this third book of my running life to a close, it is opportune to reflect not only on what the journey has meant to me personally but the effect it has had on other people's lives too. Whether by my actions and deeds, word of mouth through my running talks, or the written word through these books, the very fact that people have taken the trouble to contact me to say that I have inspired them to change their own lives for the better means as much as all the medals and trophies that decorate my shelves and walls at home.

Being a run leader, and setting other people off on what at first sight may seem a very intimidating journey, fills me with immense pride. For example, I received the following message from a wonderful lady named Norma recently, 'I really enjoyed the couch to 5k much more than I'd imagined. You've not seen the last of me!' The amazing Norma is an octogenarian. Others, having read my words or listened to my talks, have gone on to run half- and full marathons at home and overseas. And yes, a few hardy souls have ventured into the deserts and mountain trails of our world, and hold me entirely responsible!

* * *

As he tied his shoelaces on what were probably just plimsolls on that July morning back in 1981, and readied himself for that very first one-mile run, what advice would the present-day Doug give to that apprehensive earlier version of himself? The running world is not short of advice. Books, magazines, websites, personal blogs and more are all full of guidance on anything from training plans, psychology, nutrition, clothing, equipment, technology, injury prevention and treatment, but every runner knows that the most difficult part of any run is that very first step out of the door. The rest will just unfold, believe me.

Whether you are heading out for your first run, or setting out on 100-plus miles across a broiling desert, you just need to convince that little voice in your head that 'YOU CAN DOUGH IT', an inscription I now wear with pride on one of my running T-shirts!